PYTHON MASTERY

Python Mastery

A COMPREHENSIVE GUIDE FROM NOVICE TO EXPERT

Dr. Hesham Mohamed Elsherif

ELDONUSA Publishing

Contents

1 ... 1

2 PREFACE ... 3

3 WHO SHOULD READ THIS BOOK? ... 5

4 WHY THIS BOOK IS ESSENTIAL READING? ... 8

5 Introduction ... 11

6 ... 13

7 ... 15

8 Chapter 1: Introduction to Python Programming ... 17

9 Chapter 2: Control Flow and Functions ... 45

10 Chapter 3: Data Structures and Algorithms ... 60

11 Chapter 4: Object-Oriented Programming ... 88

12 Chapter 5: File Handling Operations ... 109

13 Chapter 6: Python Standard Library and Modules ... 140

14 Chapter 7: Advanced Topics in Python ... 166

15 Chapter 8: Real-World Applications and Projects ... 203

16 Chapter 9: Best Practices and Advanced Techniques ... 236

17 Chapter 10: Beyond Mastery ... 255

1

Python Mastery
A Comprehensive Guide from Novice to Expert
By
Dr. Hesham Mohamed Elsherif

ABOUT THE AUTHOR

An expert in Empirical research methodology, Dr. Elsherif special-
izes particularly in the Qualitative approach and Action research. This
specialization has not only strengthened his research endeavors but has
also allowed him to contribute invaluable insights and advancements
in these areas.

Over the years, Dr. Elsherif has made significant contributions to
the academic world not only as a professional researcher but also as an

Adjunct Professor. This multifaceted role in the educational landscape has further solidified his reputation as a thought leader and pioneer.

Furthermore, Dr. Elsherif's expertise isn't confined to one region. He has served as a consultant to numerous educational institutions on an international scale, sharing best practices, innovative strategies, and his deep insights into the ever-evolving realms of management and technology.

Combining a passion for education with an unparalleled depth of knowledge, Dr. Elsherif continues to inspire, educate, and lead in both the library and academic communities.

2

PREFACE

Welcome to Python Mastery: A Comprehensive Guide from Novice to Expert. Whether you're completely new to programming or seeking to expand your skills in one of the most powerful and versatile languages of our time, this book is crafted to be your trusted companion on your journey to mastering Python.

Python has garnered immense popularity for its simplicity, readability, and wide range of applications. From web development to data science, artificial intelligence to automation, Python serves as a cornerstone in the toolkit of modern-day programmers. Its vibrant community, rich ecosystem of libraries, and intuitive syntax make it an ideal choice for both beginners and seasoned developers alike.

In this book, we will start from the very basics of Python programming, guiding you through fundamental concepts and gradually delving into more advanced topics. Each chapter is meticulously designed to build upon the previous one, ensuring a smooth and structured learning experience.

Throughout this journey, you'll learn not only how to write code but also how to think like a Python programmer. From understanding the core principles of programming to applying advanced techniques in real-world scenarios, you'll gain the confidence and skills needed to tackle any programming challenge with ease.

What sets this book apart is its emphasis on practicality. Each concept is accompanied by clear explanations, hands-on examples, and engaging exercises to reinforce your understanding. Moreover, we'll dive into real-world applications and projects, giving you the opportunity to apply your newfound knowledge in meaningful ways.

Whether your goal is to build web applications, analyze data, or develop machine learning models, Python Mastery equips you with the tools and knowledge to turn your ideas into reality. Moreover, it instills in you the mindset of a lifelong learner, empowering you to stay curious, explore new horizons, and continually enhance your Python proficiency.

As you embark on this journey, remember that mastery is not attained overnight. It is the result of dedication, practice, and a willingness to embrace challenges. So, immerse yourself in the world of Python, embrace the joys of coding, and let this book be your guide to unlocking the full potential of your programming journey.

Thank you for choosing Python Mastery. I'm excited to accompany you on this adventure, and I look forward to seeing where your Python skills take you.

Happy coding!

Dr. Hesham Mohamed Elsherif

3

WHO SHOULD READ THIS BOOK?

Python Mastery: A Comprehensive Guide from Novice to Expert is tailored to meet the needs of a diverse audience, ranging from absolute beginners to experienced programmers looking to expand their skill set. Whether you're a student, a professional transitioning into a tech career, an entrepreneur building your own projects, or an enthusiast eager to explore the world of programming, this book is designed to cater to your learning journey.

1. **Absolute Beginners**: If you're new to programming and have little to no prior experience with coding, this book provides a gentle introduction to the world of programming using Python. We start with the basics, assuming no prior knowledge, and gradually progress to more advanced topics. You'll find clear explanations, step-by-step instructions, and ample exercises to build a solid foundation in Python programming.

2. **Students**: Whether you're studying computer science, engineering, mathematics, or any other discipline, Python Mastery serves as an invaluable companion in your academic journey. You'll

find this book to be an excellent supplement to your coursework, helping you grasp programming concepts and apply them to your assignments and projects. Moreover, the practical projects and real-world applications covered in this book offer you the opportunity to enhance your skills and showcase your abilities to potential employers or academic institutions.

3. **Career Changers**: If you're considering a career transition into the tech industry, Python Mastery equips you with the essential skills needed to pursue various roles such as software developer, data analyst, web developer, or machine learning engineer. The book covers a wide range of topics relevant to today's job market, including web development, data science, machine learning, and more. Whether you're aiming to land your first job in tech or advance your career to the next level, this book provides the knowledge and guidance to help you achieve your goals.

4. **Professionals and Developers**: Even if you're already working in the tech industry, there's always room for growth and improvement. Python Mastery offers you the opportunity to deepen your understanding of Python programming and explore advanced concepts and techniques. Whether you're looking to specialize in a particular area such as web development, data analysis, or machine learning, or you simply want to stay updated with the latest trends and best practices in Python programming, this book serves as a valuable resource for honing your skills and staying competitive in the field.

5. **Entrepreneurs and Project Managers**: If you're an entrepreneur or project manager looking to develop your own software applications or manage tech projects effectively, Python Mastery provides you with the foundational knowledge and practical insights to bring your ideas to fruition. You'll learn how to leverage Python's versatility and ecosystem of libraries to build prototypes, automate tasks, analyze data, and deploy scalable solutions. Whether you're building a startup, managing a development

team, or overseeing tech projects within your organization, this book equips you with the tools and know-how to drive success.

In summary, Python Mastery is a comprehensive guide that caters to a wide range of readers, from beginners taking their first steps into programming to experienced professionals looking to enhance their skills and advance their careers. No matter your background or aspirations, if you're eager to learn Python programming and unlock its full potential, this book is for you.

4

─────

WHY THIS BOOK IS ESSENTIAL READING?

Python Mastery: A Comprehensive Guide from Novice to Expert is not just another programming book; it's a roadmap to unlocking the full potential of Python programming and realizing your aspirations in the world of technology. Here's why this book is essential reading for anyone looking to embark on a journey of Python mastery:

Comprehensive Coverage: This book covers the entire spectrum of Python programming, from the very basics to advanced topics. Whether you're a complete beginner or an experienced programmer, you'll find relevant content and practical examples to suit your level of expertise. By following the structured learning path laid out in this book, you'll gain a deep understanding of Python and its applications across various domains.

Structured Learning Path: Python Mastery is carefully structured to guide you through a logical progression of concepts and techniques. Each chapter builds upon the previous one, ensuring that you grasp foundational concepts before moving on to more complex topics. This structured approach not only facilitates learning but also instills confidence as you advance through the book.

Practical Focus: The emphasis on practicality sets this book apart. Every concept is accompanied by real-world examples, hands-on exercises, and practical projects that reinforce your learning and demonstrate how Python is used in actual applications. Whether you're building web applications, analyzing data, or developing machine learning models, you'll find plenty of opportunities to apply your newfound knowledge in meaningful ways.

Clear Explanations: Complex topics are demystified through clear explanations and concise examples. The author employs a straightforward writing style that makes even the most challenging concepts accessible to readers of all backgrounds. Whether you're grappling with object-oriented programming or diving into advanced topics like concurrency and parallelism, you'll find the explanations in this book to be enlightening and easy to understand.

Relevance to Industry Trends: Python is at the forefront of many emerging technologies and trends, including data science, machine learning, artificial intelligence, web development, and more. By mastering Python, you position yourself at the forefront of these exciting fields, opening up a world of opportunities for career advancement and professional growth. This book equips you with the skills and knowledge needed to stay relevant in a rapidly evolving tech landscape.

Resource for Lifelong Learning: Python Mastery is not just a one-time read; it's a resource that you can return to time and again as you progress in your Python journey. Whether you're revisiting fundamental concepts for reinforcement or delving into advanced topics for deeper understanding, this book serves as a valuable companion throughout your lifelong learning journey.

Empowerment and Self-Improvement: Ultimately, this book is about empowerment and self-improvement. By mastering Python, you gain the ability to turn your ideas into reality, solve complex problems, and make a positive impact in the world. Whether you're pursuing a career in tech, starting your own business, or simply exploring your passion for programming, Python Mastery empowers you to achieve your goals and fulfill your potential.

In conclusion, Python Mastery is essential reading for anyone who is serious about mastering Python programming and harnessing its full potential. With its comprehensive coverage, structured learning path, practical focus, and relevance to industry trends, this book equips you with the knowledge and skills needed to succeed in today's technology-driven world. Whether you're a beginner taking your first steps into programming or an experienced developer looking to enhance your skills, Python Mastery is your definitive guide to Python proficiency and beyond.

Happy Reading and Learning

Dr. Hesham Mohamed Elsherif

5

Introduction

Welcome to Python Mastery, your gateway to mastering one of the most versatile and powerful programming languages in the world. Whether you're a complete beginner with no prior coding experience or an experienced developer seeking to expand your skill set, this book is designed to be your comprehensive guide on the journey from the fundamentals of Python programming to advanced concepts and techniques.

Python has emerged as a dominant force in the world of programming, renowned for its simplicity, readability, and flexibility. It is widely used across a multitude of industries and domains, including web development, data science, machine learning, artificial intelligence, automation, and more. Its popularity stems not only from its ease of learning but also from its robustness and scalability, making it a favorite among developers of all levels.

In Python Mastery, we embark on a carefully curated journey that starts with laying a solid foundation in the basics of Python programming and gradually progresses to explore more intricate and sophisticated topics. Whether you're looking to build your first Python program, dive into object-oriented programming, or tackle advanced concepts like concurrency and parallelism, this book has you covered.

Our approach is structured and systematic, ensuring that each concept is introduced in a clear and concise manner, with ample opportunities for hands-on practice and reinforcement. We believe in the importance of not just learning theory but also applying it in real-world scenarios, which is why you'll find a plethora of practical examples, exercises, and projects throughout the book.

As you embark on this journey, you'll discover the beauty and elegance of Python programming, as well as its vast capabilities and applications. You'll learn how to write clean, efficient, and Pythonic code that not only solves problems but also inspires creativity and innovation. Whether you're building websites, analyzing data, or developing cutting-edge machine learning models, Python provides you with the tools and flexibility to bring your ideas to life.

But Python Mastery is not just about acquiring technical skills; it's also about fostering a mindset of continuous learning and growth. Programming is a journey of exploration and discovery, and Python is your trusty companion along the way. As you progress through this book, we encourage you to embrace challenges, experiment with new concepts, and never stop seeking knowledge.

Whether you're aiming to kickstart a career in tech, enhance your existing skills, or simply indulge your curiosity, Python Mastery is here to support you every step of the way. So, without further ado, let's dive into the fascinating world of Python programming and embark on this exciting journey together. Welcome aboard!

6

Python stands as a towering pillar in the landscape of programming languages, revered for its unparalleled versatility, widespread adoption, and remarkable capabilities. From its humble beginnings in the late 1980s to its current status as a dominant force in the tech industry, Python has captured the hearts and minds of developers worldwide, earning a reputation as the go-to language for a diverse range of applications.

At its core, Python embodies simplicity, readability, and elegance. Unlike some of its more verbose counterparts, Python boasts a clean and intuitive syntax that closely resembles human language, making it accessible even to those with little to no programming experience. This simplicity not only accelerates the learning curve for beginners but also enhances productivity for seasoned developers, enabling them to express complex ideas with minimal code.

But simplicity is just the tip of the iceberg. What truly sets Python apart is its vast ecosystem of libraries, frameworks, and tools that empower developers to tackle virtually any task with ease. Whether you're building web applications, automating tasks, analyzing data, or developing machine learning algorithms, Python provides an extensive arsenal of resources at your fingertips, allowing you to unleash your creativity and innovate without constraints.

Moreover, Python's versatility knows no bounds. Its cross-platform compatibility means that code written in Python can seamlessly run on various operating systems, including Windows, macOS, and Linux, making it an ideal choice for developing cross-platform applications.

Additionally, Python's ability to integrate with other languages and technologies further enhances its versatility, enabling developers to leverage existing code and infrastructure to build powerful solutions.

But perhaps the most compelling aspect of Python is its community-driven ethos and ethos. From the Python Software Foundation to countless open-source contributors, Python's vibrant community is a testament to the collaborative spirit that fuels its growth and evolution. Whether you're seeking help on a programming problem, contributing to an open-source project, or attending a Python conference, you'll find a supportive and inclusive community ready to welcome you with open arms.

In this book, we embark on a journey to explore the boundless possibilities of Python programming. From the very basics of Python syntax to advanced topics like concurrency, parallelism, and beyond, we delve into the depths of Python's capabilities, equipping you with the knowledge and skills to become a proficient Python developer.

Whether you're a student embarking on your journey into the world of programming, a professional seeking to expand your skill set, or an entrepreneur looking to leverage technology to bring your ideas to life, Python has something to offer for everyone. So, join us as we unravel the mysteries of Python programming and unlock the full potential of this remarkable language. The adventure awaits!

7

Welcome to the gateway of Python mastery, where the journey of mastering one of the world's most versatile and powerful programming languages begins. Whether you're stepping into the realm of programming for the first time or seeking to elevate your skills to new heights, this book is crafted to be your unwavering companion in the pursuit of Python proficiency.

Python has earned its reputation as a cornerstone of modern programming, cherished for its simplicity, readability, and robust capabilities. Its elegant syntax and intuitive design make it an ideal starting point for beginners, while its rich ecosystem of libraries and frameworks offers boundless opportunities for seasoned developers. Regardless of your background or experience level, Python welcomes you with open arms and promises a rewarding journey of learning and growth.

In this comprehensive guide, we embark on a meticulously curated expedition through the realms of Python programming. From laying the foundational principles to exploring advanced concepts and techniques, each chapter is meticulously crafted to cater to the needs and aspirations of both beginners and experienced programmers alike.

For the complete novice, we start at square one, unraveling the mysteries of Python syntax, data types, and basic operations. Step by step, we guide you through the fundamental building blocks of programming, providing clear explanations, practical examples, and hands-on exercises to reinforce your understanding.

For the seasoned programmer seeking to deepen their expertise, we offer a treasure trove of advanced topics and techniques to explore.

Whether you're delving into object-oriented programming, mastering data structures and algorithms, or harnessing the power of Python's standard library and third-party modules, you'll find a wealth of knowledge waiting to be discovered.

But Python mastery is not just about learning syntax and techniques; it's about cultivating a mindset of continuous improvement and exploration. Throughout this journey, we encourage you to embrace challenges, experiment with new ideas, and push the boundaries of your understanding. Programming is a journey of discovery, and Python is your faithful companion in the quest for knowledge and innovation.

Whether your aspirations lie in web development, data science, artificial intelligence, or beyond, Python has something to offer for everyone. By mastering Python, you equip yourself with a powerful toolset that opens doors to a world of opportunities and possibilities.

So, whether you're embarking on your first foray into programming or seeking to ascend to new heights of expertise, let this book be your guiding light on the path to Python mastery. Together, let us embark on this exhilarating journey, where the only limit is your imagination. Welcome aboard!

8

Chapter 1: Introduction to Python Programming

Python, often hailed as the programming language for beginners, serves as an ideal entry point into the world of computer programming. In this introductory section, we embark on a journey to explore the foundational principles of Python programming, laying the groundwork for a solid understanding of its syntax, semantics, and core concepts.

Syntax and Readability: One of the defining features of Python is its clean and readable syntax, which closely resembles natural language. Python code is characterized by its use of whitespace indentation to denote code blocks, eliminating the need for cumbersome braces or semicolons. This simplicity not only makes Python code easy to write but also enhances its readability, allowing developers to focus on solving problems rather than wrestling with syntax.

Data Types and Variables: At the heart of Python programming lies the concept of data types and variables. In Python, variables are used to store data values, which can be of various types, including integers, floats, strings, lists, tuples, dictionaries, and more. Understanding how to declare variables, manipulate data types, and perform basic operations is essential for writing effective Python code.

Control Flow and Decision Making: Python offers a range of control structures, including if statements, for loops, while loops, and more, to enable decision-making and flow control within a program. By mastering these control flow mechanisms, developers gain the ability to write code that can adapt to different scenarios, execute repetitive tasks, and respond to user input.

Functions and Modularization: Functions play a crucial role in Python programming, allowing developers to encapsulate reusable pieces of code into modular units. By defining functions, developers can improve code organization, enhance readability, and promote code reuse. Additionally, Python supports the creation of user-defined functions, as well as built-in functions from the Python Standard Library, enabling developers to leverage existing functionality and extend Python's capabilities.

Input and Output Operations: Python provides robust mechanisms for handling input and output operations, allowing developers to interact with users, read from and write to files, and communicate with external systems. By mastering input/output operations in Python, developers can build interactive programs, process data from external sources, and create sophisticated applications that interact with the outside world.

Error Handling and Exceptional Situations: In the course of writing Python code, developers inevitably encounter errors and exceptional situations. Python provides a robust exception handling mechanism, allowing developers to anticipate and gracefully handle errors that may arise during program execution. By mastering error handling in Python, developers can write code that is robust, resilient, and capable of recovering gracefully from unexpected situations.

Interactive Shell and Development Environments: Python offers an interactive shell, commonly known as the Python REPL (Read-Eval-Print Loop), which allows developers to experiment with code, test ideas, and interactively explore Python's features. Additionally, Python supports a variety of development environments and tools, including text editors, Integrated Development Environments (IDEs), and online platforms, to cater to diverse preferences and workflows.

In conclusion, the introduction to Python programming serves as the gateway to a rich and rewarding journey of learning and exploration. By mastering the foundational principles of Python syntax, data types, control flow, functions, input/output operations, error handling, and development environments, developers gain the essential skills and knowledge needed to write effective Python code and embark on more advanced topics in Python programming.

Understanding The Fundamentals of Python:

At the core of Python programming lies a set of fundamental concepts that serve as the building blocks for writing code. In this section, we delve into these foundational principles, including syntax, variables, data types, and basic operations, to provide a solid understanding of Python programming.

Syntax:

Python's syntax is designed to be clear, concise, and readable, making it an ideal language for beginners and experienced programmers alike. Unlike languages that use braces or semicolons to denote code blocks, Python relies on indentation to define the structure of the code. This emphasis on whitespace ensures consistent formatting and promotes code readability. Additionally, Python supports a rich set of built-in keywords and constructs, such as if statements, for loops, while loops, and function definitions, which enable developers to express complex logic in a straightforward manner.

In the realm of programming languages, syntax acts as the grammar that dictates how code is structured and written. Python's syntax is renowned for its simplicity, readability, and elegance, making it an ideal language for beginners and experienced developers alike.

Whitespace Indentation: One of the most distinctive features of Python syntax is its use of whitespace indentation to denote code blocks. Unlike languages that rely on curly braces or keywords to delineate the beginning and end of code blocks, Python uses indentation to indicate the hierarchical structure of the code. This emphasis on consistent indentation not only enhances code readability but also enforces a clean and organized coding style.

```python
# Example of indentation in Python
if x > 5:
print("x is greater than 5")
else:
print("x is less than or equal to 5")
```

Code Blocks and Statements: In Python, code blocks are composed of one or more statements, which are individual instructions that perform specific actions. Statements are typically written on separate lines and end with a newline character. Python uses a colon (:) to indicate the beginning of a code block, followed by an indented block of code. This indentation serves to group together statements that belong to the same block.

```python
# Example of code blocks and statements in Python
if condition:
statement1
statement2
else:
statement3
statement4
```

Comments: Comments in Python are used to annotate code with explanatory notes or to disable certain portions of code during testing or debugging. Single-line comments begin with the hash symbol (#), while multi-line comments are enclosed within triple quotes (''' or """).

```python
# This is a single-line comment in Python
'''
This is a multi-line comment in Python
```

It spans multiple lines and can contain

explanatory notes or descriptions.

'''

Keywords and Identifiers: Python reserves a set of keywords that have special meanings and cannot be used as variable names or identifiers. These keywords include 'if', 'else', 'for', 'while', 'def', 'class', 'return', and many others. Identifiers, on the other hand, are names given to variables, functions, classes, and other elements in the code. Identifiers must adhere to certain rules, such as starting with a letter or underscore and consisting of letters, digits, and underscores.

Example of keywords and identifiers in Python

if condition:

variable_name = 10

function_name()

Whitespace and Line Continuation: Python is largely indifferent to whitespace within statements, allowing developers to use spaces, tabs, or a combination of both for indentation. However, consistency is key, and it is recommended to use four spaces for indentation to maintain readability. Additionally, Python allows line continuation using the backslash () character to break long lines of code into multiple lines for improved readability.

Example of line continuation in Python

result = 10 + \

20 + \

30

Understanding Python syntax is paramount to writing clean, readable, and maintainable code. By mastering the fundamental principles of Python syntax, developers can express complex ideas with clarity and precision, paving the way for efficient problem-solving and code optimization.

Variables:

In Python, variables are used to store data values, which can be of various types, including integers, floats, strings, lists, tuples, dictionaries, and more. Variables are declared by assigning a value to a name, and Python uses dynamic typing, allowing variables to change types as needed during program execution. Furthermore, Python variables are case-sensitive, meaning that 'my_variable' and 'My_Variable' are treated as distinct entities. Understanding how to declare variables, assign values, and manipulate data types is essential for writing effective Python code.

Variables serve as the building blocks of any programming language, allowing developers to store and manipulate data within a program. In Python, variables play a pivotal role in representing information, performing calculations, and facilitating communication between different parts of the code.

Declaration and Assignment: In Python, variables are declared by simply assigning a value to a name using the equals sign (=). Unlike some other programming languages, Python does not require explicit declaration of variable types. Instead, variables dynamically adopt the type of the value assigned to them at runtime.

```python
# Variable declaration and assignment in Python
x = 10
name = "John"
pi = 3.14
```

Naming Conventions: Python follows certain naming conventions for variables to ensure clarity and readability of code. Variable names should be descriptive and meaningful, conveying the purpose of the data they represent. They can contain letters, digits, and underscores, but must start with a letter or underscore. Additionally, Python uses snake_case naming convention for variables, where words are separated by underscores.

```python
# Naming conventions for variables in Python
first_name = "John"
age = 30
total_salary = 50000.50
```

Dynamic Typing: Python is dynamically typed, meaning that variables can change types during program execution. This flexibility allows developers to assign values of different types to the same variable without explicitly specifying the variable's type.

```
# Dynamic typing in Python
x = 10
x = "Hello"
```

Variable Scope: Variables in Python have a scope, which defines where in the code the variable can be accessed. There are two main types of variable scope in Python:

- Global scope: Variables defined outside of any function or class have global scope and can be accessed from anywhere in the program.
- Local scope: Variables defined within a function have local scope and can only be accessed within that function.

```
# Variable scope in Python
global_variable = 10
def my_function():
local_variable = 20
print(local_variable)
my_function()
print(global_variable)
```

Variable Reassignment: Python allows variables to be reassigned with new values at any point in the program. This feature enables developers to update variables dynamically based on changing conditions or user input.

```
# Variable reassignment in Python
x = 10
x = x + 5
```

Understanding the fundamentals of variables in Python is essential for writing clear, concise, and effective code. By mastering the concepts of variable declaration, assignment, naming conventions, scope, and dynamic typing, developers gain the foundational knowledge needed to manipulate data and solve problems in Python programming.

Data Types:

Python provides a rich set of data types to represent different kinds of data, each with its own set of operations and behaviors. Common built-in data types in Python include:

Integers:

Whole numbers without a fractional component.

In Python, data types represent the different kinds of values that can be stored and manipulated within a program. Integers, one of the fundamental data types in Python, are whole numbers without any decimal or fractional component.

Integer Declaration and Assignment: Integers in Python are declared and assigned using simple assignment statements. They can be positive, negative, or zero, and there is no limit to the size of integers in Python, allowing for arbitrarily large or small values.

```python
# Integer declaration and assignment in Python
x = 10
y = -5
z = 0
```

Arithmetic Operations: Integers support a variety of arithmetic operations, including addition (+), subtraction (-), multiplication (*), division (/), exponentiation (**), and modulus (%). These operations allow developers to perform basic mathematical calculations with integers.

```python
# Arithmetic operations with integers in Python
addition = 10 + 5 # Result: 15
subtraction = 10 - 5 # Result: 5
multiplication = 10 * 5 # Result: 50
division = 10 / 5 # Result: 2.0 (float division)
exponentiation = 2 ** 3 # Result: 8
modulus = 10 % 3 # Result: 1
```

Type Conversion: Integers can be converted to other data types using type conversion functions such as int(), float(), and str(). This allows developers to manipulate integers in different contexts or perform operations involving multiple data types.

```python
# Type conversion with integers in Python
integer_value = 10
float_value = float(integer_value) # Convert integer to float
string_value = str(integer_value) # Convert integer to string
```

Comparison Operations: Integers can be compared using comparison operators such as == (equal to), != (not equal to), < (less than), > (greater than), <= (less than or equal to), and >= (greater than or equal to). These operations allow developers to evaluate conditions and make decisions based on the values of integers.

```python
# Comparison operations with integers in Python
x = 10
y = 5
result1 = x == y # Result: False
result2 = x > y # Result: True
```

Bitwise Operations: Integers in Python also support bitwise operations, which manipulate the binary representations of integer values. Bitwise operations include bitwise AND (&), bitwise OR (|), bitwise XOR (^), bitwise NOT (~), left shift (<<), and right shift (>>). These operations are commonly used in low-level programming and cryptography.

```python
# Bitwise operations with integers in Python
x = 5 # Binary representation: 101
y = 3 # Binary representation: 011
bitwise_and = x & y # Result: 1 (binary 001)
bitwise_or = x | y # Result: 7 (binary 111)
```

Understanding the intricacies of integers in Python is essential for writing code that performs mathematical calculations, evaluates conditions, and manipulates binary data. By mastering the fundamental concepts of integer data types, developers gain the foundational knowledge needed to work with numerical data and solve a wide range of computational problems.

Floats:

Numbers with a fractional component, represented with a decimal point.

In Python, floats represent numbers with decimal points or fractions. As one of the fundamental data types, floats play a crucial role in various mathematical computations and scientific applications.

Float Declaration and Assignment: Floats in Python are declared and assigned using decimal numbers, optionally with a decimal point or exponent notation. They can represent both positive and negative numbers, as well as fractions.

Float declaration and assignment in Python

x = 3.14

y = -0.5

z = 1.0e3 # Scientific notation (1.0 x 10^3)

Arithmetic Operations: Floats support a wide range of arithmetic operations, including addition (+), subtraction (-), multiplication (*), division (/), exponentiation (**), and modulus (%). These operations enable developers to perform complex mathematical calculations involving decimal numbers.

Arithmetic operations with floats in Python

addition = 3.14 + 2.5 # Result: 5.64

subtraction = 3.14 - 2.5 # Result: 0.64

multiplication = 3.14 * 2.5 # Result: 7.85

division = 3.14 / 2.5 # Result: 1.256

exponentiation = 2 ** 3.14 # Result: 8.8249778270076287

Precision and Floating Point Arithmetic: Floats in Python are represented using the IEEE 754 standard for floating-point arithmetic. However, due to the inherent limitations of binary floating-point representation, floats may not always be able to represent decimal numbers precisely. This can lead to rounding errors and inaccuracies in calculations involving floats.

Floating point precision in Python

x = 0.1 + 0.2

print(x) # Result: 0.30000000000000004 (not exactly 0.3)

Type Conversion: Floats can be converted to other data types using type conversion functions such as int() and str(). This allows developers to manipulate floats in different contexts or perform operations involving multiple data types.

Type conversion with floats in Python

float_value = 3.14

integer_value = int(float_value) # Convert float to integer

string_value = str(float_value) # Convert float to string

Comparison Operations: Floats can be compared using comparison operators such as ==, !=, <, >, <=, and >=. However, due to the limitations of floating-point arithmetic, direct comparison of floats for equality may lead to unexpected results. Instead, it is recommended to use tolerance-based comparison or compare floats within a certain range.

Comparison operations with floats in Python

x = 3.14

y = 3.15

result1 = x == y # Result: False

result2 = x < y # Result: True

Understanding the nuances of floats in Python is essential for writing code that performs accurate numerical calculations and handles decimal numbers with precision. By mastering the fundamental concepts of float data types, developers gain the foundational knowledge needed to work with numerical data effectively and develop robust scientific and mathematical applications.

Strings:

Sequences of characters enclosed within single quotes, double quotes, or triple quotes.

Strings are an essential data type in Python used to represent textual data. They allow developers to manipulate and process sequences of characters, making them invaluable for tasks such as text processing, manipulation, and formatting.

String Declaration and Assignment: Strings in Python are declared by enclosing text within single quotes (' '), double quotes (" "), or triple quotes (''' '''). This flexibility allows developers to include quotes within strings and create multi-line strings.

```python
# String declaration and assignment in Python
name = 'John'
message = "Hello, World!"
multi_line_string = '''This is a
multi-line string.'''
```

String Concatenation: Strings in Python can be concatenated using the plus (+) operator. This operation allows developers to combine multiple strings into a single string.

```python
# String concatenation in Python
first_name = 'John'
last_name = 'Doe'
full_name = first_name + ' ' + last_name
```

String Indexing and Slicing: Strings in Python are indexed using zero-based indexing, allowing developers to access individual characters or substrings within a string. Additionally, strings support slicing, which enables developers to extract substrings based on specified start and end indices.

```python
# String indexing and slicing in Python
message = "Hello, World!"
first_character = message[0] # Accessing the first character ('H')
substring = message[7:12] # Extracting substring 'World'
```

String Methods: Python provides a rich set of built-in methods for manipulating strings. These methods allow developers to perform operations such as converting case, stripping whitespace, splitting and joining strings, replacing substrings, and more.

```python
# String methods in Python
message = "Hello, World!"
```

uppercase_message = message.upper() # Convert to uppercase

stripped_message = message.strip() # Remove leading and trailing whitespace

split_message = message.split(',') # Split string into a list based on delimiter

String Formatting: Python offers multiple approaches for formatting strings, including %-formatting, str.format() method, and f-strings (formatted string literals). These techniques allow developers to insert variables and expressions into strings in a readable and flexible manner.

String formatting in Python

name = 'John'

age = 30

formatted_string = 'My name is %s and I am %d years old.' % (name, age)

Escape Sequences: Python supports escape sequences, which are special characters preceded by a backslash () that represent non-printable or special characters. Common escape sequences include '\n' (newline), '\t' (tab), '\"' (double quote), '\'' (single quote), and '\\' (backslash).

Escape sequences in Python strings

message = "This is a \n multi-line \n string."

Understanding the intricacies of strings in Python is essential for handling textual data effectively and performing various text processing tasks. By mastering the fundamental concepts of string data types, developers gain the foundational knowledge needed to manipulate and process strings in Python programming.

Lists:

Ordered collections of elements, mutable and heterogeneous.

Lists are a versatile and fundamental data type in Python used to store collections of items. They allow developers to organize, manipulate, and iterate over sequences of data, making them indispensable for a wide range of programming tasks.

List Declaration and Initialization: Lists in Python are declared by enclosing comma-separated values within square brackets ([]). They can contain elements of different data types, including integers, floats, strings, and even other lists.

```python
# List declaration and initialization in Python
numbers = [1, 2, 3, 4, 5]
names = ['John', 'Jane', 'Alice']
mixed_list = [1, 'Hello', 3.14, True]
```

Accessing Elements: Elements in a list can be accessed using zero-based indexing. Additionally, negative indices can be used to access elements from the end of the list. List slicing allows developers to extract sublists based on specified start and end indices.

```python
# Accessing elements and list slicing in Python
numbers = [1, 2, 3, 4, 5]
first_element = numbers[0] # Accessing the first element (1)
last_element = numbers[-1] # Accessing the last element (5)
sublist = numbers[2:4] # Extracting sublist [3, 4]
```

Modifying Lists: Lists in Python are mutable, meaning that their elements can be modified after creation. Developers can update, add, remove, and insert elements into a list using various list methods and operations.

```python
# Modifying lists in Python
numbers = [1, 2, 3, 4, 5]
numbers[2] = 10 # Update element at index 2
numbers.append(6) # Add element to the end of the list
numbers.remove(3) # Remove element from the list
numbers.insert(2, 7) # Insert element at index 2
```

List Operations: Python provides a variety of list operations, including concatenation, repetition, membership testing, length calculation, and sorting. These operations enable developers to manipulate lists efficiently and perform common tasks with ease.

```python
# List operations in Python
list1 = [1, 2, 3]
```

```
list2 = [4, 5, 6]
concatenated_list = list1 + list2 # Concatenation
repeated_list = list1 * 3 # Repetition
is_present = 3 in list1 # Membership testing
list_length = len(list1) # Length calculation
sorted_list = sorted(list1) # Sorting
```

List Comprehensions: List comprehensions provide a concise and elegant way to create lists based on existing lists or other iterable objects. They allow developers to express transformations, filters, and combinations of elements in a compact and readable syntax.

```
# List comprehensions in Python
numbers = [1, 2, 3, 4, 5]
squared_numbers = [x ** 2 for x in numbers] # Square each element
even_numbers = [x for x in numbers if x % 2 == 0] # Select even numbers
```

Understanding the intricacies of lists in Python is essential for organizing data, performing iterative operations, and implementing algorithms efficiently. By mastering the fundamental concepts of list data types, developers gain the foundational knowledge needed to work with collections of data effectively in Python programming.

Tuples:

Ordered collections of elements, immutable and heterogeneous.

Tuples are immutable sequences in Python, often used to store collections of heterogeneous data. They are similar to lists but have a few key differences, primarily their immutability and syntax.

Tuple Declaration and Initialization: Tuples in Python are declared by enclosing comma-separated values within parentheses (). Unlike lists, tuples are immutable, meaning their elements cannot be modified after creation.

```
# Tuple declaration and initialization in Python
person = ('John', 30, 'Male')
coordinates = (3.14, 2.71)
empty_tuple = ()
```

Accessing Elements: Elements in a tuple can be accessed using zero-based indexing, similar to lists. Tuples support slicing, allowing developers to extract sub-tuples based on specified start and end indices.

```python
# Accessing elements and tuple slicing in Python
person = ('John', 30, 'Male')
name = person[0] # Accessing the first element ('John')
age_gender = person[1:] # Extracting a sub-tuple (30, 'Male')
```

Immutability: Tuples are immutable, meaning their elements cannot be modified, added, or removed after creation. Once a tuple is initialized, its elements remain fixed, making tuples suitable for representing data that should not change over time.

```python
# Immutable nature of tuples in Python
coordinates = (3.14, 2.71)
coordinates[0] = 2.0 # Raises TypeError: 'tuple' object does not support item assignment
```

Tuple Operations: While tuples are immutable, they support various operations such as concatenation, repetition, membership testing, and length calculation. These operations allow developers to manipulate tuples and perform common tasks efficiently.

```python
# Tuple operations in Python
tuple1 = (1, 2, 3)
tuple2 = (4, 5, 6)
concatenated_tuple = tuple1 + tuple2 # Concatenation
repeated_tuple = tuple1 * 3 # Repetition
is_present = 3 in tuple1 # Membership testing
tuple_length = len(tuple1) # Length calculation
```

Tuple Unpacking: Tuples support unpacking, a feature that allows developers to assign the elements of a tuple to multiple variables in a single statement. This feature is particularly useful for extracting values from tuples and assigning them to meaningful variable names.

```python
# Tuple unpacking in Python
person = ('John', 30, 'Male')
```

name, age, gender = person # Unpacking the tuple into variables

Immutable Collections: Tuples are commonly used to represent immutable collections of data, such as coordinates, configurations, and records. Their immutability ensures data integrity and prevents accidental modification.

Using tuples for immutable collections in Python

coordinates = (3.14, 2.71)

config = ('DEBUG', 'localhost', 8080)

Understanding the nuances of tuples in Python is essential for working with immutable data collections and designing robust, efficient programs. By mastering the fundamental concepts of tuple data types, developers gain the foundational knowledge needed to leverage tuples effectively in Python programming.

Dictionaries:

Unordered collections of key-value pairs, mutable and heterogeneous.

Dictionaries are versatile data structures in Python that allow developers to store collections of key-value pairs. They provide a flexible and efficient way to organize and manipulate data, enabling fast lookups and retrieval of values based on keys

Dictionary Declaration and Initialization: Dictionaries in Python are declared by enclosing key-value pairs within curly braces ({}) and separating them with colons (:). Each key-value pair is separated by a comma (,). Dictionaries can contain keys and values of any data type, allowing for flexible data organization.

Dictionary declaration and initialization in Python

person = {'name': 'John', 'age': 30, 'gender': 'Male'}

student = {'id': 12345, 'name': 'Alice', 'grades': [85, 90, 95]}

empty_dict = {}

Accessing and Modifying Elements: Elements in a dictionary are accessed using keys rather than indices. Dictionaries support fast lookups, allowing developers to retrieve values based on their associated keys. Values can be added, updated, or removed from a dictionary using assignment statements or built-in methods.

```python
# Accessing and modifying elements in a dictionary
person = {'name': 'John', 'age': 30, 'gender': 'Male'}
name = person['name'] # Accessing value associated with the key 'name'
person['age'] = 31 # Updating value associated with the key 'age'
del person['gender'] # Removing key-value pair with the key 'gender'
```

Dictionary Operations: Dictionaries support various operations, including membership testing, length calculation, key retrieval, value retrieval, and iteration. These operations allow developers to manipulate dictionaries and perform common tasks efficiently.

```python
# Dictionary operations in Python
person = {'name': 'John', 'age': 30, 'gender': 'Male'}
is_present = 'age' in person # Membership testing
dict_length = len(person) # Length calculation
keys = person.keys() # Retrieving keys
values = person.values() # Retrieving values
```

Dictionary Methods: Python provides a rich set of built-in methods for working with dictionaries. These methods allow developers to add, update, remove, and manipulate key-value pairs, as well as perform operations such as copying, merging, and clearing dictionaries.

```python
# Dictionary methods in Python
person = {'name': 'John', 'age': 30, 'gender': 'Male'}
person.update({'city': 'New York'}) # Adding key-value pair
person.pop('age') # Removing key-value pair
person.clear() # Clearing all key-value pairs
```

Dictionary Comprehensions: Similar to list comprehensions, dictionary comprehensions provide a concise and elegant way to create dictionaries based on existing dictionaries or other iterable objects. They allow developers to express transformations and filters of key-value pairs in a compact syntax.

```python
# Dictionary comprehensions in Python
```

```python
numbers = [1, 2, 3, 4, 5]
squared_numbers = {x: x ** 2 for x in numbers} # Square each
```
number and create a dictionary

Key Immunity: Keys in a dictionary must be unique and immutable, meaning they cannot be modified after creation. Common immutable data types used as keys include strings, integers, floats, and tuples.

```python
# Using immutable keys in dictionaries in Python
student_grades = {(1, 'Math'): 85, (1, 'Science'): 90, (2, 'Math'): 95}
```

Understanding the intricacies of dictionaries in Python is essential for organizing and manipulating structured data effectively. By mastering the fundamental concepts of dictionary data types, developers gain the foundational knowledge needed to leverage dictionaries efficiently in Python programming.

Basic Operations:

Python supports a wide range of basic operations for performing arithmetic, string manipulation, and data manipulation. These operations include addition, subtraction, multiplication, division, exponentiation, modulus, concatenation, slicing, indexing, and more.

In Python programming, basic operations encompass a wide range of fundamental actions that developers perform to manipulate data, control program flow, and perform computations. These operations are essential building blocks for writing effective and efficient code.

Arithmetic Operations: Arithmetic operations involve mathematical calculations such as addition (+), subtraction (-), multiplication (*), division (/), exponentiation (**), and modulus (%). These operations allow developers to perform numerical computations and manipulate numeric data.

```python
# Arithmetic operations in Python
result_addition = 5 + 3 # Addition
result_subtraction = 5 - 3 # Subtraction
result_multiplication = 5 * 3 # Multiplication
result_division = 5 / 3 # Division
result_exponentiation = 5 ** 3 # Exponentiation
```

result_modulus = 5 % 3 # Modulus

Comparison Operations: Comparison operations involve comparing two values and determining their relationship. Common comparison operators include equal to (==), not equal to (!=), greater than (>), less than (<), greater than or equal to (>=), and less than or equal to (<=). These operations return Boolean values (True or False) based on the comparison result.

```
# Comparison operations in Python
result_equal = 5 == 3 # Equal to
result_not_equal = 5 != 3 # Not equal to
result_greater_than = 5 > 3 # Greater than
result_less_than = 5 < 3 # Less than
result_greater_than_or_equal = 5 >= 3 # Greater than or equal to
result_less_than_or_equal = 5 <= 3 # Less than or equal to
```

Logical Operations: Logical operations involve combining Boolean values using logical operators such as AND (and), OR (or), and NOT (not). These operations allow developers to perform logical comparisons and make decisions based on multiple conditions.

```
# Logical operations in Python
condition1 = True
condition2 = False
result_and = condition1 and condition2 # Logical AND
result_or = condition1 or condition2 # Logical OR
result_not = not condition1 # Logical NOT
```

Assignment Operations: Assignment operations involve assigning values to variables using the assignment operator (=). Python also supports augmented assignment operators such as +=, -=, *=, /=, //=, %=, **=, which combine arithmetic operations with assignment.

```
# Assignment operations in Python
x = 5 # Simple assignment
x += 3 # Augmented assignment (equivalent to x = x + 3)
```

Membership and Identity Operations: Python provides membership operators (in, not in) and identity operators (is, is not) for testing membership and identity relationships between objects. Membership operators are used to check if a value exists in a sequence, while identity operators are used to compare the memory address of two objects.

Membership and identity operations in Python

sequence = [1, 2, 3, 4, 5]

result_membership = 3 in sequence # Membership testing

result_identity = x is None # Identity testing

Understanding and mastering these basic operations are essential for writing clear, concise, and effective Python code. By mastering the fundamental concepts of basic operations, developers gain the foundational knowledge needed to manipulate data, control program flow, and solve a wide range of computational problems in Python programming.

Additionally, Python provides shorthand operators, such as +=, -=, *=, /=, to perform in-place modifications of variables. Understanding how to perform basic operations in Python is fundamental to writing code that can effectively solve problems and accomplish tasks.

By mastering the fundamentals of Python programming, including syntax, variables, data types, and basic operations, developers gain the essential skills and knowledge needed to write clear, concise, and effective Python code. These foundational concepts serve as the bedrock upon which more advanced topics and techniques in Python programming are built, empowering developers to tackle increasingly complex challenges with confidence and proficiency.

Setting Up Your Python Environment:

Setting up your Python environment is the first step towards embarking on your journey into Python programming. This involves installing Python, choosing an Integrated Development Environment (IDE) or text editor, and getting started with coding.

Installing Python:

- Python can be downloaded and installed from the official Python website (https://www.python.org/).
- On the website, navigate to the Downloads section and choose the appropriate installer for your operating system (Windows, macOS, or Linux).
- Follow the installation instructions provided on the website or included in the installer to complete the installation process.
- During installation, ensure that the option to add Python to the system PATH is selected. This allows you to run Python from the command line or terminal.

1. **Choosing an IDE**:
   - An Integrated Development Environment (IDE) is a software application that provides comprehensive facilities for programming, debugging, and code editing in one unified interface.
   - There are several popular IDEs available for Python development, each with its own set of features and benefits. Some popular choices include:
     - PyCharm: A powerful IDE developed by JetBrains with features such as code analysis, debugging, and version control integration.
     - Visual Studio Code (VS Code): A lightweight and versatile code editor with a wide range of extensions available for Python development.
     - Jupyter Notebook: An interactive notebook environment for Python programming, widely used for data science and research.
   - Choose an IDE that best suits your needs, preferences, and workflow. You can try out multiple IDEs to find the one that works best for you.
2. **Getting Started with Coding**:
   - Once Python is installed and your IDE is set up, you're ready to start coding.

- Open your chosen IDE and create a new Python file (usually with a .py extension) to write your code.
- Begin by writing simple Python scripts to familiarize yourself with the language syntax, variables, data types, and basic operations.
- Experiment with writing code snippets, running them, and observing the output to understand how Python works.
- Explore Python documentation, tutorials, and online resources to learn more about Python programming concepts, best practices, and advanced topics.

3. **Additional Considerations**:
   - Virtual Environments: Consider using virtual environments (such as venv or virtualenv) to manage project dependencies and isolate project environments. This helps avoid conflicts between different Python projects and ensures reproducibility.
   - Package Management: Familiarize yourself with Python package management tools such as pip, which allows you to install, upgrade, and manage Python packages and dependencies.
   - Version Control: Consider using version control systems such as Git and hosting platforms like GitHub or GitLab to manage and collaborate on your Python projects.

Setting up your Python environment is a crucial step that lays the foundation for your Python programming journey. By installing Python, choosing an IDE, and getting started with coding, you'll be well-equipped to explore the vast possibilities of Python programming and develop your skills as a Python developer.

Writing Your First Python Program:

Introduction to Python Programming: Writing Your First Python Program

Congratulations on taking your first steps into the world of Python programming! Writing your first Python program is an exciting milestone that marks the beginning of your journey into the world of coding.

1. **Hello, World!:**
    - The traditional "Hello, World!" program is a simple yet iconic introductory program that prints the message "Hello, World!" to the screen.
    - Open your preferred text editor or Integrated Development Environment (IDE) and create a new Python file.
    - Type the following code into your file:

```
# hello_world.py
print("Hello, World!")
```

- Save the file with a .py extension, such as hello_world.py.
- Open a terminal or command prompt, navigate to the directory containing your Python file, and run the program by entering the following command:

```
python hello_world.py
```

- You should see the output "Hello, World!" printed to the terminal.

1. **Beyond "Hello, World!":**
    - Now that you've written your first Python program, it's time to explore beyond the basics and dive deeper into Python programming.
    - Experiment with variables, data types, and basic operations to perform calculations and manipulate data.

- ○ Explore control flow statements such as if statements, for loops, and while loops to control the flow of your programs based on conditions.
- ○ Learn about functions and how to define and call functions to modularize your code and make it more reusable.
- ○ Dive into more advanced topics such as object-oriented programming, file handling, exception handling, and working with external libraries and modules.
- ○ Consider working on small projects or exercises to apply what you've learned and reinforce your understanding of Python programming concepts.
- ○ Take advantage of online resources, tutorials, and documentation to continue learning and exploring new aspects of Python programming.

2. **Practical Examples**:

- ○ As you progress in your Python journey, consider working on practical examples and projects to apply your skills in real-world scenarios.

  Examples of practical projects include:

  - Building a simple calculator program that performs basic arithmetic operations.
  - Creating a text-based game or interactive story using user input and conditional statements.
  - Developing a web scraper to extract data from websites or APIs.
  - Writing scripts to automate repetitive tasks, such as file management or data processing.
  - Exploring data analysis and visualization by working with datasets and plotting libraries such as matplotlib or seaborn.

Writing your first Python program is just the beginning of an exciting and rewarding journey into the world of programming. By starting with "Hello, World!" and exploring beyond, you'll gain the foundational knowledge and skills needed to tackle more advanced topics and embark on a wide range of coding projects. So, embrace the learning process, stay curious, and enjoy the journey ahead as you dive deeper into Python programming.

Exploring Python's Interactive Shell:

Python's interactive shell provides a powerful and convenient way to experiment with code snippets, test Python syntax, and explore the behavior of Python constructs in real-time.

Accessing the Interactive Shell:

- Python's interactive shell, also known as the Python interpreter or REPL (Read-Evaluate-Print Loop), can be accessed from the command line or terminal.
- Open a terminal or command prompt on your computer and type **python** to launch the Python interpreter.
- You should see the Python prompt >>>, indicating that the interpreter is ready to accept Python code input.

1. **Exploring Python Syntax:**
    - The interactive shell allows you to experiment with Python syntax and language features in real-time.
    - Start by typing simple Python expressions, statements, and commands directly into the shell and observe the output.
    - For example, you can perform arithmetic calculations, define variables, create data structures, and call built-in functions:

```
>>> 5 + 3 # Addition
8
>>> x = 10 # Variable assignment
>>> x * 2 # Multiplication
```

```
20
>>> my_list = [1, 2, 3] # List creation
>>> len(my_list) # Calling a built-in function
3
```

Interactive Code Experimentation:

- The interactive shell allows you to experiment with code snippets interactively, making it a valuable tool for learning and exploring Python.
- Try out different Python constructs, control flow statements, and language features to see how they behave in real-time.
- Use the shell to debug code snippets, test hypotheses, and understand the behavior of Python expressions and statements.
- For example, you can test conditional statements, iterate over sequences, define functions, and interact with objects:

```
>>> if x > 5:
... print("x is greater than 5")
... else:
... print("x is not greater than 5")
...
x is greater than 5
>>> for item in my_list:
... print(item)
...
1
2
3
>>> def square(x):
... return x ** 2
...
>>> square(4)
16
```

Exploring Module and Package Imports:

- You can import modules and packages directly into the interactive shell to explore their contents and functionality.
- Use the **import** statement followed by the module or package name to import it into the shell.
- Once imported, you can access the attributes, functions, and classes defined in the module or package and experiment with them:

```
>>> import math # Import the math module
>>> math.sqrt(25) # Calculate the square root
5.0
```

Exiting the Interactive Shell:

- To exit the interactive shell, type **exit()** or press **Ctrl + D** (Unix/ Linux) or **Ctrl + Z** followed by **Enter** (Windows).
- You'll return to the command prompt or terminal from which you launched the Python interpreter.

The interactive shell is an invaluable tool for Python developers of all levels, from beginners to experienced programmers. Use it to experiment with code snippets, test Python syntax, and explore Python's vast ecosystem of libraries and packages. By leveraging the interactive shell, you'll gain hands-on experience with Python programming and accelerate your learning journey in Python.

9

Chapter 2: Control Flow and Functions

Control flow and functions are fundamental concepts in Python programming that enable developers to control the execution flow of their code and organize it into reusable, modular components.

Conditional Statements:

- Conditional statements allow developers to execute different blocks of code based on specified conditions.
- The **if, elif** (else if), and **else** keywords are used to define conditional statements in Python.
- Conditional statements can be used to make decisions and control the flow of program execution based on the evaluation of Boolean expressions.

```python
# Example of conditional statements in Python
x = 10
if x > 5:
print("x is greater than 5")
elif x == 5:
```

```
print("x is equal to 5")
else:
print("x is less than 5")
```

Loops:

- Loops allow developers to execute a block of code repeatedly, either a fixed number of times or until a specified condition is met.
- Python supports two main types of loops: **for** loops and **while** loops.
- **for** loops are typically used for iterating over sequences (such as lists, tuples, or strings), while **while** loops are used for executing a block of code repeatedly until a condition becomes false.

```
# Example of loops in Python
# Using a for loop to iterate over a list
numbers = [1, 2, 3, 4, 5]
for number in numbers:
print(number)
# Using a while loop to print numbers from 1 to 5
i = 1
while i <= 5:
print(i)
i += 1
```

Functions:

- Functions are reusable blocks of code that perform a specific task or calculation.
- Functions help in organizing code, improving readability, and promoting code reusability.
- Functions are defined using the **def** keyword followed by the function name, parameters (if any), and a colon (:). The body of

the function is indented and contains the code to be executed when the function is called.

```python
# Example of defining and calling a function in Python
def greet(name):
"""Function to greet a person by name"""
print("Hello, " + name + "!")
# Calling the greet function
greet("Alice")
```

Returning Values from Functions:

- Functions can return values using the **return** statement.
- When a function returns a value, it can be assigned to a variable or used in other expressions.

```python
# Example of returning values from functions in Python
def add(x, y):
"""Function to add two numbers"""
return x + y
# Calling the add function and storing the result in a variable
result = add(3, 5)
print("Result:", result)
```

Function Parameters:

- Functions can accept parameters, which are variables passed to the function when it is called. Parameters allow functions to accept input values and operate on them.
- Parameters can have default values, allowing functions to be called with fewer arguments.

```python
# Example of function parameters in Python
def power(base, exponent=2):
"""Function to calculate the power of a number"""
```

```
return base ** exponent
# Calling the power function with different arguments
print("2 to the power of 3:", power(2, 3))
print("3 squared:", power(3))
```

Control flow constructs and functions are essential tools in Python programming for implementing logic, controlling program execution, and organizing code into reusable components. By mastering these concepts, developers can write more efficient, maintainable, and scalable Python code for a wide range of applications.

Learning About Control Structures:

Control structures are fundamental components of any programming language, including Python. They allow developers to control the flow of execution in their code, make decisions based on conditions, and perform repetitive tasks efficiently.

1. **If Statements**:
   - If statements allow developers to execute different blocks of code based on specified conditions.
   - The syntax of an if statement consists of the **if** keyword followed by a condition, followed by a colon (:), and an indented block of code to be executed if the condition evaluates to True.
   - Optionally, an if statement can include **elif** (else if) and **else** clauses to define additional conditions and code blocks to execute if the previous conditions are not met.

```
# Example of if statement in Python
x = 10
if x > 5:
print("x is greater than 5")
elif x == 5:
```

```
print("x is equal to 5")
else:
print("x is less than 5")
```

If statements are foundational control structures in Python programming that allow developers to execute different blocks of code based on specified conditions.

1. **Syntax**:

    ○ The syntax of an if statement in Python is straightforward:

```
if condition:
# Code block to execute if condition is True
```

Usage:

- If statements are used to make decisions based on conditions, allowing programs to respond dynamically to different scenarios.
- Conditions in if statements are typically Boolean expressions that evaluate to either True or False.
- The code block following the if statement is executed only if the condition evaluates to True. If the condition is False, the code block is skipped.

```
# Example of using if statement in Python
x = 10
if x > 5:
print("x is greater than 5")
```

lif and else Clauses:

- In addition to the if statement, Python provides **elif** (else if) and **else** clauses to handle multiple conditions.
- The **elif** clause is used to check additional conditions if the previous condition(s) are False.

- The **else** clause is optional and is executed if none of the previous conditions are True.

```python
# Example of using elif and else clauses in Python
x = 10
if x > 10:
print("x is greater than 10")
elif x == 10:
print("x is equal to 10")
else:
print("x is less than 10")
```

Nested If Statements:

- If statements can be nested within each other to handle more complex conditions.
- Nested if statements allow for finer-grained control over program flow, but excessive nesting can lead to code that is difficult to read and understand.

```python
# Example of nested if statements in Python
x = 10
if x > 5:
print("x is greater than 5")
if x < 15:
print("x is less than 15")
```

Best Practices:

- Keep if statements concise and focused on a single condition or logical branch.
- Use meaningful variable names and conditions to enhance code readability.
- Use comments to document complex conditions or explain the purpose of if statements.

- Avoid excessive nesting of if statements to prevent code from becoming overly complex and difficult to maintain.

If statements are essential tools in Python programming for making decisions and controlling the flow of program execution. By mastering if statements and understanding their syntax, usage, and best practices, developers can write more efficient, readable, and maintainable code that responds dynamically to different scenarios and conditions.

Loops:

- Loops are used to execute a block of code repeatedly, either a fixed number of times or until a specified condition is met.
- Python supports two main types of loops: **for** loops and **while** loops.
- **for** loops are typically used for iterating over sequences (such as lists, tuples, or strings), while **while** loops are used for executing a block of code repeatedly until a condition becomes false.

```python
# Example of loops in Python
# Using a for loop to iterate over a list
numbers = [1, 2, 3, 4, 5]
for number in numbers:
print(number)
# Using a while loop to print numbers from 1 to 5
i = 1
while i <= 5:
print(i)
i += 1
```

Logical Operators:

- Logical operators are used to combine multiple conditions in if statements and loops.
- Python supports three main logical operators: **and**, **or**, and **not**.

- These operators allow developers to create complex conditions by combining simpler conditions using logical conjunctions and disjunctions.

```
# Example of logical operators in Python
x = 10
y = 20
if x > 5 and y < 30:
print("Both conditions are True")
if x > 15 or y < 15:
print("At least one condition is True")
if not x == 0:
print("x is not equal to 0")
```

Understanding control structures such as if statements, loops, and logical operators is essential for writing Python code that can make decisions, iterate over data, and perform complex operations. By mastering these control structures, developers can write more flexible, efficient, and readable code that meets the requirements of various programming tasks and scenarios.

Defining And Calling Functions in Python:

Functions are essential building blocks in Python programming that allow developers to encapsulate reusable blocks of code, making programs more modular, organized, and maintainable.

Defining Functions:

- Functions in Python are defined using the **def** keyword followed by the function name, parentheses () containing any parameters, and a colon (:).
- The body of the function is indented and contains the code to be executed when the function is called.

```
# Example of defining a function in Python
```

```python
def greet(name):
"""Function to greet a person by name"""
print("Hello, " + name + "!")
```

Calling Functions:

- Functions are called or invoked by using the function name followed by parentheses () containing any arguments or parameters required by the function.
- When a function is called, the code inside the function's body is executed, and any specified parameters are passed to the function.

```python
# Example of calling a function in Python
greet("Alice")
```

Function Parameters:

- Parameters are variables that are defined in the function's signature and receive values when the function is called.
- Parameters allow functions to accept input values and operate on them.
- Parameters can have default values, allowing functions to be called with fewer arguments.

```python
# Example of function parameters with default values in Python
def power(base, exponent=2):
"""Function to calculate the power of a number"""
return base ** exponent
# Calling the power function with different arguments
print("2 to the power of 3:", power(2, 3))
print("3 squared:", power(3))
```

Return Values:

- Functions can return values using the **return** statement. The return statement terminates the function and returns the specified value(s) to the caller.
- When a function returns a value, it can be assigned to a variable or used in other expressions.

```python
# Example of returning values from a function in Python
def add(x, y):
"""Function to add two numbers"""
return x + y
# Calling the add function and storing the result in a variable
result = add(3, 5)
print("Result:", result)
```

Function Scope:

- Variables defined inside a function have local scope, meaning they are only accessible within the function.
- Variables defined outside of any function have global scope, meaning they are accessible throughout the entire program.
- Local variables take precedence over global variables with the same name within the function's scope.

```python
# Example of function scope in Python
global_var = 10
def my_function():
local_var = 20
print("Local variable:", local_var)
print("Global variable:", global_var)
my_function()
```

Understanding how to define and call functions, work with parameters and return values, and manage variable scope is essential for writing modular and maintainable Python code. By leveraging functions effectively, developers can create reusable blocks of code that promote code organization, readability, and efficiency.

Mastering The Concept of Recursion:

Recursion is a powerful programming technique in which a function calls itself in order to solve a problem. It's a fundamental concept in computer science and has numerous applications in Python programming.

Understanding Recursion:

- Recursion is based on the idea of breaking down a problem into smaller, similar subproblems, and solving each subproblem recursively until a base case is reached.
- A base case is a condition where the function stops calling itself and returns a result directly, without further recursion.
- Recursion involves two main components: the base case and the recursive case.

Example of Recursion:

- The classic example of recursion is computing the factorial of a non-negative integer.
- The factorial of a non-negative integer n (denoted as n!) is the product of all positive integers less than or equal to n.
- The recursive definition of factorial is:
    - n! = n * (n-1)!
- Here's how this recursive definition can be implemented in Python:

```python
# Example of factorial computation using recursion in Python
def factorial(n):
if n == 0:
return 1 # Base case: factorial of 0 is 1
else:
return n * factorial(n - 1) # Recursive case
# Test the factorial function
print("Factorial of 5:", factorial(5)) # Output: 120
```

Applications of Recursion:

- Recursion is widely used in various programming tasks and algorithms, including:
  - Tree and graph traversal algorithms (e.g., depth-first search, breadth-first search).
  - Sorting algorithms (e.g., merge sort, quicksort).
  - Solving mathematical problems (e.g., computing Fibonacci numbers, solving Towers of Hanoi).
  - Parsing and processing hierarchical data structures (e.g., XML, JSON).
  - Generating permutations and combinations.

Benefits and Trade-offs of Recursion:

- Recursion offers several benefits, including:
  - Simplifying complex problems by breaking them down into smaller, manageable subproblems.
  - Writing elegant and concise code that closely mirrors the problem's mathematical or structural properties.
- However, recursion may also have trade-offs, such as:
  - Increased memory usage due to the function call stack, which can lead to stack overflow errors for deeply nested recursive calls.
  - Potentially slower performance compared to iterative solutions for certain problems.

Best Practices for Recursion:

- Ensure that the recursive function has a base case to prevent infinite recursion.
- Ensure that each recursive call makes progress toward the base case to avoid infinite recursion.
- Consider the memory usage and potential performance implications when using recursion, especially for large inputs or deeply nested recursive calls.
- Use recursion judiciously and consider alternative iterative solutions for problems where recursion may not be the most efficient approach.

By mastering the concept of recursion and understanding its applications in Python programming, developers can tackle a wide range of problems more effectively and elegantly. Recursion provides a powerful tool for solving complex problems and implementing efficient algorithms, making it an essential skill for any Python programmer.

Exploring Lambda Functions:

In addition to traditional function definitions, Python offers powerful tools for working with functions, including lambda functions, function decorators, and advanced function techniques. These features provide flexibility and expressiveness in writing concise and efficient code.

Lambda Functions:

- Lambda functions, also known as anonymous functions, are small, inline functions defined using the **lambda** keyword.
- Lambda functions are often used for simple, one-line operations where defining a named function would be overkill.
- The syntax of a lambda function is: **lambda parameters: expression**.
- Lambda functions can take any number of parameters but can only contain a single expression, which is evaluated and returned.

```
# Example of a lambda function in Python
add = lambda x, y: x + y
print(add(3, 5)) # Output: 8
```

Function Decorators:

- Function decorators are higher-order functions that modify or enhance the behavior of other functions.

- Decorators are typically used to add additional functionality to functions without modifying their original implementation.
- Decorators are implemented using the @ syntax followed by the decorator function's name above the function definition.
- Decorator functions typically accept a function as input, perform some processing, and return a new function or modify the existing function's behavior.

```python
# Example of a function decorator in Python
def uppercase_decorator(func):
def wrapper(*args, **kwargs):
result = func(*args, **kwargs)
return result.upper()
return wrapper
@uppercase_decorator
def greet(name):
return f"Hello, {name}!"
print(greet("Alice")) # Output: HELLO, ALICE!
```

Advanced Function Techniques:

- Python provides several advanced techniques for working with functions, including:
    - Variable-length argument lists: Functions can accept a variable number of positional arguments (*args) and keyword arguments (**kwargs) using tuple and dictionary unpacking.
    - Nested functions: Functions can be defined within other functions, allowing for hierarchical code organization and scoping.
    - Closure: Inner functions (nested functions) can capture and retain the enclosing function's local state even after the enclosing function has finished executing.
    - Currying: The process of converting a function with multiple arguments into a sequence of functions, each taking

a single argument, allowing for partial application of arguments.

```python
# Example of advanced function techniques in Python
def add(*args):
return sum(args)
def multiply(factor):
def wrapper(*args):
return factor * add(*args)
return wrapper
double = multiply(2)
print(double(3, 5)) # Output: 16 (2 * (3 + 5) = 16)
```

Exploring lambda functions, function decorators, and advanced function techniques in Python opens up new possibilities for writing concise, expressive, and powerful code. By leveraging these features, developers can create more flexible and efficient solutions to a wide range of programming problems, enhancing code readability and maintainability in the process.

10

Chapter 3: Data Structures and Algorithms

Data structures and algorithms are fundamental concepts in computer science and play a crucial role in software development. They provide the foundation for organizing, storing, and manipulating data efficiently, as well as solving computational problems effectively.

Understanding Data Structures:

- Data structures are specialized formats for organizing, storing, and managing data in computer memory.
- They define the relationship between data elements, allowing for efficient access, retrieval, and manipulation of data.
- Common types of data structures include arrays, linked lists, stacks, queues, trees, graphs, hash tables, and sets.
- Each data structure has its own characteristics, advantages, and limitations, making it suitable for specific tasks and scenarios.

Exploring Algorithms:

- Algorithms are step-by-step procedures or instructions for solving computational problems.

- They define the logic and operations needed to accomplish a specific task or achieve a desired outcome.
- Algorithms can be categorized based on their purpose, complexity, and design paradigm (e.g., sorting, searching, graph traversal, dynamic programming).
- Well-designed algorithms are efficient, scalable, and robust, providing optimal solutions to various problems within acceptable time and resource constraints.

Applications of Data Structures and Algorithms:

- Data structures and algorithms are ubiquitous in computer science and have numerous applications across different domains, including:
    - Information retrieval and search engines: Efficient data structures (e.g., hash tables, trees) and algorithms (e.g., binary search, indexing) power search engines to retrieve relevant information quickly.
    - Database management systems: Data structures such as B-trees and algorithms for query optimization enable efficient storage and retrieval of data in databases.
    - Operating systems: Data structures (e.g., queues, stacks) and scheduling algorithms manage system resources, process scheduling, and memory allocation in operating systems.
    - Networking and routing: Graph data structures and algorithms (e.g., Dijkstra's algorithm, Bellman-Ford algorithm) are used for routing and network optimization in computer networks.
    - Artificial intelligence and machine learning: Data structures (e.g., matrices, tensors) and algorithms (e.g., neural networks, clustering algorithms) underpin various AI and ML models and algorithms.

Importance of Data Structures and Algorithms:

- Data structures and algorithms form the backbone of software development and computer science education.

- They enable efficient problem-solving, algorithmic thinking, and optimization of software performance.
- Understanding data structures and algorithms is essential for writing efficient, scalable, and maintainable code, as well as for succeeding in technical interviews and competitions.

Challenges and Best Practices:

- Designing and implementing efficient data structures and algorithms require careful consideration of various factors, including time complexity, space complexity, and practical constraints.
- It's essential to choose the right data structure and algorithm for a given problem based on its requirements, constraints, and expected usage patterns.
- Continuously improving algorithmic skills through practice, learning from others, and staying updated with advancements in the field is crucial for mastering data structures and algorithms.

In conclusion, data structures and algorithms are essential pillars of computer science and software engineering, providing the necessary tools and techniques for organizing, processing, and analyzing data efficiently. By understanding the principles, types, and applications of data structures and algorithms, developers can write more efficient code, solve complex problems effectively, and advance their careers in technology.

Understanding Data Structures:

Data structures are fundamental components in programming languages that allow for the efficient organization, storage, and manipulation of data. In Python, several built-in data structures serve different purposes and have unique characteristics.

Lists:

- Lists are ordered collections of items, allowing for the storage of multiple elements in a single variable.

- Lists are mutable, meaning their elements can be modified after creation.
- Elements in a list can be of different data types, and they can be accessed using indices.
- Common operations on lists include appending, inserting, removing, slicing, and iterating over elements.

```python
# Example of a list in Python
my_list = [1, 2, 3, 'a', 'b', 'c']
print(my_list[0]) # Output: 1
my_list.append(4)
print(my_list) # Output: [1, 2, 3, 'a', 'b', 'c', 4]
```

Tuples:

- Tuples are ordered collections of items, similar to lists, but they are immutable.
- Once created, the elements in a tuple cannot be changed, added, or removed.
- Tuples are often used to represent fixed collections of data, such as coordinates, constants, or database records.
- Tuple elements can be accessed using indices, and tuple packing and unpacking are common operations.

```python
# Example of a tuple in Python
my_tuple = (1, 2, 3, 'a', 'b', 'c')
print(my_tuple[0]) # Output: 1
```

Dictionaries:

- Dictionaries are unordered collections of key-value pairs, allowing for efficient lookup and retrieval of values based on keys.
- Keys in a dictionary must be unique and immutable (e.g., strings, numbers, tuples), while values can be of any data type.
- Dictionaries are mutable, meaning their elements can be modified, added, or removed.

- Common operations on dictionaries include accessing, inserting, updating, and deleting key-value pairs.

```
# Example of a dictionary in Python
my_dict = {'name': 'John', 'age': 30, 'city': 'New York'}
print(my_dict['name']) # Output: John
my_dict['age'] = 31
print(my_dict) # Output: {'name': 'John', 'age': 31, 'city': 'New York'}
```

Sets:

- Sets are unordered collections of unique elements, ensuring that each element appears only once.
- Sets are mutable, allowing for the addition and removal of elements, but they do not support indexing.
- Sets support mathematical set operations such as union, intersection, difference, and symmetric difference.

```
# Example of a set in Python
my_set = {1, 2, 3, 4, 5}
my_set.add(6)
print(my_set) # Output: {1, 2, 3, 4, 5, 6}
```

Best Use Cases:

- Lists are suitable for ordered collections of elements where duplicates are allowed and the order matters.
- Tuples are ideal for immutable collections of elements where the order is significant and elements cannot be changed.
- Dictionaries are optimal for unordered collections of key-value pairs, offering efficient lookup and retrieval based on keys.
- Sets are valuable for unordered collections of unique elements, providing support for set operations and efficient membership testing.

Understanding the properties, operations, and best use cases of lists, tuples, dictionaries, and sets is essential for effective data manipulation and algorithm design in Python. By leveraging these built-in data structures appropriately, developers can write more efficient, scalable, and maintainable code for a wide range of applications.

The following is more explanation for each structure:

Lists:

Lists are one of the most commonly used data structures in Python, offering a versatile and flexible way to store collections of items.

Properties of Lists:

- Lists are ordered collections of items, allowing for the storage of multiple elements in a single variable.
- Lists can contain elements of different data types, including integers, floats, strings, and even other lists.
- Lists are mutable, meaning their elements can be modified, added, or removed after creation.
- Lists are zero-indexed, meaning elements can be accessed using indices starting from 0 for the first element.

Creating Lists:

- Lists in Python are created by enclosing a comma-separated sequence of elements within square brackets **[]**.
- Empty lists can be created using empty square brackets or by using the **list()** constructor.

```python
# Example of creating lists in Python
my_list = [1, 2, 3, 'a', 'b', 'c']
empty_list = []
```

Accessing Elements:

- Elements in a list can be accessed using square brackets **[]** and indices.

- Negative indices can be used to access elements from the end of the list.
- Slicing can be used to extract sublists from a list using the syntax **[start:end:step]**.

```python
# Example of accessing elements in a list
print(my_list[0]) # Output: 1
print(my_list[-1]) # Output: 'c'
print(my_list[2:5]) # Output: [3, 'a', 'b']
```

Common Operations:

- Lists support various operations for manipulation and traversal, including:
    - Appending and extending lists using the **append()** and **extend()** methods.
    - Inserting elements at specific positions using the **insert()** method.
    - Removing elements by value using the **remove()** method or by index using the **pop()** method.
    - Checking for the presence of elements using the **in** keyword.
    - Iterating over elements using loops (e.g., **for** loop) or list comprehensions.

```python
# Example of common operations on lists
my_list.append(4) # Append element to the end of the list
my_list.extend([5, 6]) # Extend list with another list
my_list.insert(2, 'x') # Insert element at index 2
my_list.remove('a') # Remove first occurrence of 'a'
popped_element = my_list.pop(0) # Remove and return element at index 0
```

Best Practices:

- Use meaningful variable names to represent lists and their elements.
- Avoid modifying a list while iterating over it to prevent unexpected behavior.
- Take advantage of list comprehensions for concise and efficient list creation and manipulation.
- Consider using built-in functions such as **len()**, **min()**, **max()**, and **sum()** for common list operations.
- Keep in mind the time complexity of list operations (e.g., appending vs. inserting) for performance-critical code.

Lists are powerful and versatile data structures in Python, offering a wide range of operations for storing and manipulating collections of items. By understanding the properties, operations, and best practices for using lists effectively, developers can write more efficient and maintainable code for various applications and scenarios.

Tuples:

Tuples are another essential data structure in Python, offering ordered collections of elements similar to lists, but with some key differences.

Properties of Tuples:

- Tuples are ordered collections of elements, allowing for the storage of multiple items in a single variable.
- Tuples are immutable, meaning their elements cannot be changed, added, or removed after creation.
- Tuples can contain elements of different data types, similar to lists.
- Tuples are zero-indexed, allowing elements to be accessed using indices starting from 0 for the first element.

Creating Tuples:

- Tuples in Python are created by enclosing a comma-separated sequence of elements within parentheses ().

- Empty tuples can be created using empty parentheses or by using the **tuple()** constructor.

```
# Example of creating tuples in Python
my_tuple = (1, 2, 3, 'a', 'b', 'c')
empty_tuple = ()
```

Accessing Elements:

- Elements in a tuple can be accessed using square brackets [] and indices, similar to lists.
- Negative indices can be used to access elements from the end of the tuple.
- Slicing can be used to extract sub-tuples from a tuple using the syntax **[start:end:step]**.

```
# Example of accessing elements in a tuple
print(my_tuple[0]) # Output: 1
print(my_tuple[-1]) # Output: 'c'
print(my_tuple[2:5]) # Output: (3, 'a', 'b')
```

Common Operations:

- While tuples are immutable and cannot be modified directly, they support various operations for traversal and manipulation, including:
  - Checking for the presence of elements using the **in** keyword.
  - Iterating over elements using loops (e.g., **for** loop).
  - Concatenating tuples using the + operator.
  - Replicating tuples using the * operator.
  - Unpacking tuples to assign their elements to variables.

```
# Example of common operations on tuples
if 'a' in my_tuple:
```

```
print("Element 'a' is present in the tuple")
for element in my_tuple:
print(element)
concatenated_tuple = my_tuple + (4, 5, 6)
replicated_tuple = my_tuple * 2
x, y, z, *rest = my_tuple # Unpacking tuple elements
```

Best Practices:

- Use tuples for collections of elements that should not change after creation, such as constant values or function return values.
- Take advantage of tuple packing and unpacking to simplify code and improve readability.
- Use tuples as keys in dictionaries when the order of elements matters and the elements are immutable.
- Document the meaning and usage of tuples using descriptive variable names and comments.

Tuples are lightweight, immutable data structures in Python that provide a convenient way to represent fixed collections of elements. By understanding the properties, operations, and best practices for using tuples effectively, developers can write more concise, efficient, and maintainable code for various applications and scenarios.

Dictionaries

Dictionaries are versatile and powerful data structures in Python, providing a flexible way to store and retrieve data using key-value pairs.

Properties of Dictionaries:

- Dictionaries are unordered collections of key-value pairs, allowing for efficient lookup and retrieval of values based on keys.
- Keys in a dictionary must be unique and immutable (e.g., strings, numbers, tuples), while values can be of any data type.

- Dictionaries are mutable, meaning their elements can be modified, added, or removed after creation.
- Dictionaries are highly optimized for fast retrieval of values based on keys, making them ideal for building mappings and associative arrays.

Creating Dictionaries:

- Dictionaries in Python are created by enclosing a comma-separated sequence of key-value pairs within curly braces {}.
- Key-value pairs are separated by colons : with keys and values separated by commas.

```python
# Example of creating dictionaries in Python
my_dict = {'name': 'John', 'age': 30, 'city': 'New York'}
empty_dict = {}
```

Accessing and Modifying Elements:

- Elements in a dictionary can be accessed using square brackets [] and keys.
- Values can be modified, added, or removed using assignment, the **update()** method, or the **del** keyword.

```python
# Example of accessing and modifying elements in a dictionary
print(my_dict['name']) # Output: John
my_dict['age'] = 31 # Modify value for key 'age'
my_dict['gender'] = 'Male' # Add new key-value pair
del my_dict['city'] # Remove key-value pair for key 'city'
```

Common Operations:

Dictionaries support various operations for manipulation and traversal, including:

- Checking for the presence of keys using the **in** and **not in** keywords.
- Getting the number of key-value pairs in a dictionary using the **len()** function.
- Iterating over keys, values, or key-value pairs using loops (e.g., **for** loop) or dictionary methods.
- Merging dictionaries using the **update()** method or dictionary unpacking.

```python
# Example of common operations on dictionaries
if 'name' in my_dict:
print("Key 'name' is present in the dictionary")
for key in my_dict:
print(key, my_dict[key])
merged_dict = {'country': 'USA', **my_dict} # Dictionary unpacking
```

Best Practices:

- Use meaningful and descriptive keys to represent data in dictionaries.
- Document the meaning and usage of keys and values using comments or docstrings.
- Handle missing keys gracefully using techniques such as the **get()** method or the **defaultdict** class from the **collections** module.
- Consider the time complexity of dictionary operations (e.g., lookup, insertion) for performance-critical code.

Dictionaries are versatile and efficient data structures in Python that provide a convenient way to represent mappings and associative arrays. By understanding the properties, operations, and best practices for using dictionaries effectively, developers can write more concise, readable, and maintainable code for various applications and scenarios.

Sets:

Sets are a fundamental data structure in Python that represent unordered collections of unique elements.

Properties of Sets:

- Sets are unordered collections of distinct elements, meaning each element appears only once in the set.
- Sets do not allow duplicate elements, ensuring that each element is unique.
- Sets are mutable, meaning elements can be added or removed after creation.
- Sets can contain elements of different data types, and elements are not ordered.

Creating Sets:

- Sets in Python are created by enclosing a comma-separated sequence of elements within curly braces {}.
- Alternatively, the **set()** constructor can be used to create an empty set or convert other iterable objects (e.g., lists, tuples) to sets.

```
# Example of creating sets in Python
my_set = {1, 2, 3, 4, 5}
empty_set = set()
```

Accessing and Modifying Elements:

- Elements in a set cannot be accessed using indices because sets are unordered.
- Elements can be added to a set using the **add()** method or removed using the **remove()** or **discard()** methods.
- Sets also support other set operations such as union, intersection, difference, and symmetric difference.

```
# Example of modifying elements in a set
```

my_set.add(6) # Add element to the set
my_set.remove(3) # Remove element from the set

Common Operations:

- Sets support various operations for manipulation and set arithmetic, including:
    - Checking for the presence of elements using the **in** keyword.
    - Performing set operations such as union, intersection, difference, and symmetric difference using operators (|, **&**, -, ^) or set methods (**union()**, **intersection()**, **difference()**, **symmetric_difference()**).
    - Iterating over elements using loops (e.g., **for** loop) or set comprehensions.

```
# Example of common operations on sets
if 5 in my_set:
print("Element 5 is present in the set")
other_set = {4, 5, 6, 7}
union_set = my_set | other_set # Union of two sets
intersection_set = my_set & other_set # Intersection of two sets
difference_set = my_set - other_set # Difference of two sets
symmetric_difference_set = my_set ^ other_set # Symmetric difference of two sets
```

Best Practices:

- Use sets when dealing with collections of unique elements and performing set operations.
- Keep in mind that sets do not maintain element order, so if order matters, consider using other data structures like lists or tuples.
- Be cautious when modifying a set while iterating over it to prevent unexpected behavior.

- Take advantage of set comprehensions for concise and efficient set creation and manipulation.

Sets are efficient and versatile data structures in Python that provide a convenient way to work with collections of unique elements and perform set operations. By understanding the properties, operations, and best practices for using sets effectively, developers can write more concise, readable, and efficient code for various applications and scenarios.

Implementing Common Algorithms:

Python's rich set of built-in data structures provides a solid foundation for implementing various algorithms efficiently.

Sorting Algorithms:

- Python's built-in **sorted()** function and the **sort()** method of lists can be used to implement sorting algorithms such as:
  - Bubble Sort
  - Selection Sort
  - Insertion Sort
  - Merge Sort
  - Quick Sort

```
# Example of sorting using Python's built-in functions
my_list = [5, 3, 8, 1, 2, 4]
sorted_list = sorted(my_list) # Using sorted()
my_list.sort() # Using sort() method
```

Searching Algorithms:

- Python's built-in data structures like lists and dictionaries can be used to implement searching algorithms such as:
  - Linear Search

- ○ Binary Search
- ○ Hashing (using dictionaries)

```python
# Example of searching using Python's built-in data structures
def linear_search(arr, target):
for i, num in enumerate(arr):
if num == target:
return i
return -1
def binary_search(arr, target):
left, right = 0, len(arr) - 1
while left <= right:
mid = (left + right) // 2
if arr[mid] == target:
return mid
elif arr[mid] < target:
left = mid + 1
else:
right = mid - 1
return -1
```

Graph Traversal Algorithms:

- Python's dictionaries and sets can be used to represent graphs and implement traversal algorithms such as:
  - ○ Depth-First Search (DFS)
  - ○ Breadth-First Search (BFS)

```python
# Example of graph traversal using Python's data structures
def dfs(graph, node, visited=None):
if visited is None:
visited = set()
visited.add(node)
for neighbor in graph[node]:
if neighbor not in visited:
```

```
dfs(graph, neighbor, visited)
return visited
def bfs(graph, start):
visited = set()
queue = [start]
while queue:
node = queue.pop(0)
if node not in visited:
visited.add(node)
queue.extend(graph[node])
return visited
```

Dynamic Programming Algorithms:

- Python's lists or dictionaries can be used to implement dynamic programming algorithms for solving optimization problems efficiently, such as:
    - Fibonacci sequence
    - Longest Common Subsequence (LCS)
    - Knapsack problem

```
# Example of dynamic programming using Python's data structures
def fibonacci(n, memo={}):
if n in memo:
return memo[n]
if n <= 2:
return 1
memo[n] = fibonacci(n-1, memo) + fibonacci(n-2, memo)
return memo[n]
```

By leveraging Python's versatile data structures such as lists, dictionaries, and sets, along with its rich set of built-in functions and methods, developers can implement a wide range of algorithms efficiently. Understanding how to utilize Python's data structures effectively can lead to concise, readable, and optimized algorithm implementations for solving various computational problems.

Exploring More Advanced Data Structures:

While Python provides a rich set of built-in data structures like lists, tuples, dictionaries, and sets, there are more advanced data structures that can be leveraged for solving complex problems efficiently.

1. **Linked Lists**:
   - Linked lists are linear data structures where elements are stored in nodes, each containing a reference to the next node in the sequence.
   - Linked lists can be singly linked (each node points to the next node) or doubly linked (each node points to both the next and previous nodes).
   - Linked lists are particularly useful for dynamic memory allocation and implementing other data structures like stacks and queues.

2. **Trees**:
   - Trees are hierarchical data structures consisting of nodes connected by edges, where each node has a parent and zero or more children.
   - Common types of trees include binary trees (each node has at most two children), binary search trees (BST), AVL trees, and red-black trees.
   - Trees are widely used in computer science for organizing hierarchical data, implementing search algorithms, and representing abstract syntax trees (ASTs) in compilers.

3. **Graphs**:
   - Graphs are non-linear data structures consisting of vertices (nodes) connected by edges (links), representing relationships between objects.
   - Graphs can be directed (edges have a direction) or undirected (edges have no direction) and can have weighted edges representing the cost or distance between vertices.

- ○ Graphs are used in various applications such as social networks, network routing, recommendation systems, and geographic information systems (GIS).

4. **Heaps**:

- ○ Heaps are specialized tree-based data structures that satisfy the heap property, where the value of each parent node is greater than or equal to (max heap) or less than or equal to (min heap) the values of its children.
- ○ Heaps are commonly used to implement priority queues, where elements are dequeued in order of priority based on their value.

5. **Hash Tables**:

- ○ Hash tables, also known as hash maps or dictionaries in Python, are data structures that store key-value pairs and provide efficient lookup, insertion, and deletion operations.
- ○ Hash tables use a hash function to map keys to indices in an array, allowing for constant-time average-case access.

6. **Trie**:

- ○ Trie (pronounced "try") is a tree-based data structure used for storing a dynamic set of strings where each node represents a common prefix of its children.
- ○ Tries are efficient for tasks like autocomplete, spell checking, and dictionary implementations, where fast prefix-based search operations are required.

7. **Graphical Structures**:

- ○ Other advanced data structures include graphical structures such as segment trees, quad trees, and k-d trees, which are used for spatial indexing, range queries, and nearest neighbor searches in multidimensional data.

Exploring these advanced data structures expands the toolkit available to developers for solving complex computational problems efficiently. By understanding the properties, operations, and applications of these data structures, developers can design more optimized algorithms and build robust software systems capable of handling diverse data and computational tasks.

Stacks:

Stacks are dynamic data structures that follow the Last In, First Out (LIFO) principle, meaning the last element added to the stack is the first one to be removed. Stacks are widely used in computer science and software engineering for various applications.

Properties of Stacks:

- Stacks are collections of elements with two main operations: push and pop.
- The push operation adds an element to the top of the stack, while the pop operation removes the top element.
- Stacks can be implemented using arrays or linked lists, with arrays offering constant-time access to elements but limited capacity, and linked lists providing dynamic memory allocation but potentially slower access.

Common Operations:

- Apart from push and pop, stacks support other operations such as peek, isEmpty, and size.
- The peek operation retrieves the top element of the stack without removing it.
- The isEmpty operation checks if the stack is empty, while the size operation returns the number of elements in the stack.

Applications of Stacks:

- Stacks find applications in various areas of computer science and software engineering, including:

- ○ Function call stack: Stacks are used by programming languages to manage function calls and local variables.
- ○ Expression evaluation: Stacks are employed in parsing and evaluating arithmetic expressions, infix to postfix conversion, and evaluating postfix expressions.
- ○ Backtracking algorithms: Stacks are used in backtracking algorithms such as depth-first search (DFS) to keep track of visited nodes and backtrack when necessary.
- ○ Undo mechanisms: Stacks can be utilized to implement undo mechanisms in text editors, graphical user interfaces, and other applications where users need to revert actions.
- ○ Memory management: Stacks play a crucial role in managing memory allocation and deallocation in operating systems and programming languages.

Implementation:

- Stacks can be implemented using arrays or linked lists in Python. Here's an example of a stack implemented using a Python list:

```python
class Stack:
def __init__(self):
self.stack = []
def push(self, item):
self.stack.append(item)
def pop(self):
if not self.isEmpty():
return self.stack.pop()
else:
raise IndexError("Stack is empty")
def peek(self):
if not self.isEmpty():
return self.stack[-1]
else:
```

```
return None
def isEmpty(self):
return len(self.stack) == 0
def size(self):
return len(self.stack)
```

By understanding the properties, operations, and applications of stacks, developers can effectively utilize this versatile data structure to solve a wide range of problems efficiently. Stacks play a vital role in algorithm design and implementation, offering a simple yet powerful tool for managing data in various contexts.

Queues:

Queues are dynamic data structures that follow the First In, First Out (FIFO) principle, meaning the first element added to the queue is the first one to be removed. Queues are fundamental in computer science and are utilized in various applications.

Properties of Queues:

- Queues are collections of elements with two primary operations: enqueue and dequeue.
- The enqueue operation adds an element to the rear (end) of the queue, while the dequeue operation removes the element at the front (front) of the queue.
- Queues can be implemented using arrays or linked lists, with arrays offering constant-time access to elements but limited capacity, and linked lists providing dynamic memory allocation but potentially slower access.

Common Operations:

- Apart from enqueue and dequeue, queues support other operations such as peek, isEmpty, and size.
- The peek operation retrieves the element at the front of the queue without removing it.

- The isEmpty operation checks if the queue is empty, while the size operation returns the number of elements in the queue.

Applications of Queues:

- Queues find applications in various areas of computer science and software engineering, including:
    - Task scheduling: Queues are used to schedule tasks in operating systems, network routers, and job queues in distributed computing systems.
    - Breadth-First Search (BFS): Queues are employed in BFS traversal algorithms for graph traversal, level-order traversal in trees, and shortest path algorithms.
    - Print queue management: Queues are used in print spoolers to manage print jobs in the order they are received.
    - Message queues: Queues are utilized in message-oriented middleware systems for asynchronous communication between distributed components.
    - CPU scheduling: Queues are used in CPU scheduling algorithms to manage processes waiting to be executed.

Implementation:

- Queues can be implemented using arrays or linked lists in Python. Here's an example of a queue implemented using a Python list:

```python
class Queue:
def __init__(self):
self.queue = []
def enqueue(self, item):
self.queue.append(item)
def dequeue(self):
if not self.isEmpty():
return self.queue.pop(0)
```

```
else:
raise IndexError("Queue is empty")
def peek(self):
if not self.isEmpty():
return self.queue[0]
else:
return None
def isEmpty(self):
return len(self.queue) == 0
def size(self):
return len(self.queue)
```

By understanding the properties, operations, and applications of queues, developers can effectively utilize this versatile data structure to solve a wide range of problems efficiently. Queues play a vital role in algorithm design and implementation, offering a simple yet powerful tool for managing data in various contexts.

Graphs:

Graphs are fundamental data structures that represent relationships between objects. They consist of a set of vertices (nodes) connected by edges (links). Graphs can model various real-world scenarios and are extensively used in computer science and related fields.

Properties of Graphs:

- Vertices: Nodes representing entities or objects.
- Edges: Links connecting pairs of vertices, representing relationships between them.
- Directed vs. Undirected: In directed graphs (digraphs), edges have a direction, while in undirected graphs, edges have no direction.
- Weighted vs. Unweighted: In weighted graphs, edges have associated weights or costs, while in unweighted graphs, all edges have the same weight.

Types of Graphs:

- Directed Graphs (Digraphs): Each edge has a direction, indicating a one-way relationship between vertices.
- Undirected Graphs: Edges have no direction, and relationships between vertices are bidirectional.
- Weighted Graphs: Edges have associated weights, representing the cost or distance between vertices.
- Acyclic Graphs: Graphs with no cycles, meaning there are no paths that lead back to the same vertex.
- Cyclic Graphs: Graphs containing cycles, where there exists a path that leads back to the same vertex.

Representations of Graphs:

- Adjacency Matrix: A 2D array where the presence or absence of an edge between vertices is indicated by 1 or 0, respectively. Weighted graphs can use the weight value instead of 1.
- Adjacency List: Each vertex maintains a list of adjacent vertices, representing the edges connected to it. This representation is more memory-efficient for sparse graphs.
- Edge List: A list of tuples or objects representing edges, containing the source and destination vertices along with optional weight information.

Graph Traversal Algorithms:

- Depth-First Search (DFS): Explores as far as possible along each branch before backtracking. Useful for topological sorting, cycle detection, and connected components.
- Breadth-First Search (BFS): Explores all vertices at the current depth level before moving to the next level. Useful for shortest path algorithms, connected components, and level-order traversal.

Applications of Graphs:

- Social Networks: Modeling friendships, connections, and interactions between individuals.

- Network Routing: Finding the shortest path or optimal route between network nodes.
- Recommendation Systems: Recommending products, services, or content based on user interactions and preferences.
- Compiler Design: Representing program structure and dependencies in abstract syntax trees (ASTs).
- Geographic Information Systems (GIS): Modeling spatial relationships between geographical features.

1. **Graph Algorithms**:
    - Shortest Path Algorithms: Finding the shortest path between two vertices, such as Dijkstra's algorithm and Bellman-Ford algorithm.
    - Minimum Spanning Tree (MST): Finding the minimum-weight connected subtree that spans all vertices in the graph, such as Prim's algorithm and Kruskal's algorithm.
    - Topological Sorting: Ordering vertices in a directed acyclic graph (DAG) such that for every directed edge uv from vertex u to vertex v, u comes before v in the ordering.
    - Cycle Detection: Identifying cycles or loops in a graph, which is essential for ensuring data consistency and avoiding infinite loops.

Analyzing Algorithm Efficiency:

Efficiency is a crucial aspect of algorithm design, as it determines how well an algorithm performs in terms of time and space requirements. Analyzing the efficiency of algorithms involves evaluating their time complexity and space complexity, which provide insights into how the algorithm's performance scales with input size.

Time Complexity:

- Time complexity measures the amount of time an algorithm takes to execute as a function of the input size.

- It provides an estimation of the worst-case scenario, indicating how the algorithm's runtime grows with larger inputs.
- Time complexity is typically expressed using Big O notation, representing the upper bound on the growth rate of the algorithm's runtime.

Example time complexity classes:

- $O(1)$: Constant time complexity, where the runtime remains constant regardless of the input size.
- $O(\log n)$: Logarithmic time complexity, common in algorithms like binary search, where the runtime grows logarithmically with the input size.
- $O(n)$: Linear time complexity, where the runtime grows linearly with the input size.
- $O(n^2)$: Quadratic time complexity, common in algorithms like nested loops, where the runtime grows quadratically with the input size.
- $O(2^n)$: Exponential time complexity, indicating an algorithm that grows exponentially with the input size.

Space Complexity:

- Space complexity measures the amount of memory an algorithm consumes as a function of the input size.
- It includes both the memory required for storing input data and any additional memory used during algorithm execution, such as auxiliary data structures.
- Like time complexity, space complexity is typically expressed using Big O notation, representing the upper bound on memory usage.

Example space complexity classes:

- $O(1)$: Constant space complexity, indicating that the algorithm uses a fixed amount of memory regardless of input size.
- $O(n)$: Linear space complexity, where the memory usage scales linearly with the input size.

- O(n^2): Quadratic space complexity, common in algorithms that use nested data structures or matrices.

Importance of Analyzing Efficiency:

- Efficiency analysis helps identify bottlenecks in algorithms and optimize them for better performance.
- It enables comparison between different algorithms for solving the same problem, aiding in algorithm selection.
- Understanding time and space complexity allows developers to make informed decisions about algorithm design and implementation.

Techniques for Analyzing Efficiency:

- Counting operations: Analyzing the number of basic operations (e.g., comparisons, assignments) performed by the algorithm as a function of input size.
- Recurrence relations: Using mathematical equations to describe the runtime of recursive algorithms and solving them to determine time complexity.
- Worst-case analysis: Considering the scenario that maximizes the algorithm's runtime to derive an upper bound on time complexity.
- Space usage analysis: Examining the memory consumption of the algorithm, including variables, data structures, and recursive calls.

Efficient algorithms are critical for optimizing resource usage and improving system performance. By analyzing time complexity and space complexity, developers can design algorithms that scale well with input size and meet performance requirements for a wide range of applications.

11

Chapter 4: Object-Oriented Programming

Object-Oriented Programming (OOP) is a programming paradigm that revolves around the concept of objects, which are instances of classes. Python is an object-oriented programming language that fully supports OOP principles

Classes and Objects:

- A class is a blueprint for creating objects. It defines the attributes (properties) and methods (functions) that objects of that class will have.
- An object is an instance of a class, representing a specific entity or concept in the program.
- Classes and objects allow for a modular and organized way to structure code, facilitating code reuse and maintenance.

```python
# Example of a simple class definition in Python
class Car:
```

```python
def __init__(self, brand, model):
self.brand = brand
self.model = model
def drive(self):
print(f"Driving {self.brand} {self.model}")
# Creating objects (instances) of the Car class
car1 = Car("Toyota", "Camry")
car2 = Car("Honda", "Civic")
```

Attributes and Methods:

- Attributes are variables associated with objects, representing their state or properties.
- Methods are functions associated with objects, representing their behavior or actions.
- Attributes and methods are accessed using dot notation (**object.attribute** or **object.method()**).

Inheritance:

- Inheritance allows a class (subclass) to inherit attributes and methods from another class (superclass).
- Subclasses can extend or override the functionality of their superclass.
- Python supports single inheritance (one subclass inherits from one superclass) and multiple inheritance (one subclass inherits from multiple superclasses).

```python
# Example of inheritance in Python
class ElectricCar(Car):
def __init__(self, brand, model, battery_capacity):
super().__init__(brand, model)
self.battery_capacity = battery_capacity
def charge(self):
```

```python
print(f"Charging {self.brand} {self.model}")
```

Encapsulation:

- Encapsulation is the bundling of data (attributes) and methods that operate on that data within a single unit (class).
- It allows for data hiding, preventing direct access to internal attributes from outside the class.
- Access to attributes and methods is controlled using access specifiers like public, private, and protected.

```python
# Example of encapsulation in Python
class BankAccount:
def __init__(self, account_number, balance):
self._account_number = account_number # Protected attribute
self.__balance = balance # Private attribute
def deposit(self, amount):
self.__balance += amount
def withdraw(self, amount):
if amount <= self.__balance:
self.__balance -= amount
else:
print("Insufficient funds")
```

Polymorphism:

- Polymorphism allows objects of different classes to be treated as objects of a common superclass.
- It enables methods to behave differently based on the type of object they operate on, enhancing flexibility and modularity.

```python
# Example of polymorphism in Python
class Animal:
def sound(self):
pass
class Dog(Animal):
```

```python
def sound(self):
print("Woof")
class Cat(Animal):
def sound(self):
print("Meow")
def make_sound(animal):
animal.sound()
dog = Dog()
cat = Cat()
make_sound(dog) # Output: Woof
make_sound(cat) # Output: Meow
```

Object-Oriented Programming in Python provides a powerful mechanism for organizing and structuring code, enhancing code reusability, maintainability, and scalability. By understanding and applying OOP principles, developers can design modular, flexible, and robust software solutions for a wide range of applications.

Introduction To Object-Oriented Programming:

Object-Oriented Programming (OOP) is a programming paradigm that emphasizes the organization of code into objects, which are instances of classes. Python fully supports OOP principles and provides powerful features for defining classes, creating objects, and implementing inheritance.

Classes:

- A class is a blueprint for creating objects. It defines the attributes (data) and methods (functions) that objects of that class will have.
- Classes provide a way to encapsulate related data and behavior, promoting code reusability and modularity.
- In Python, classes are defined using the **class** keyword followed by the class name, and the class body is typically indented.

```python
# Example of a simple class definition in Python
```

```python
class Car:
def __init__(self, brand, model):
self.brand = brand
self.model = model
def drive(self):
print(f"Driving {self.brand} {self.model}")
```

Objects:

- An object is an instance of a class, representing a specific entity or concept in the program.
- Objects encapsulate data (attributes) and behavior (methods) defined by their class.
- Multiple objects can be created from the same class, each with its own unique state.

```python
# Creating objects (instances) of the Car class
car1 = Car("Toyota", "Camry")
car2 = Car("Honda", "Civic")
```

Inheritance:

- Inheritance is a mechanism by which a class (subclass) can inherit attributes and methods from another class (superclass).
- Subclasses can extend or override the functionality of their superclass.
- In Python, inheritance is achieved by placing the name of the superclass in parentheses after the subclass name in the class definition.

```python
# Example of inheritance in Python
class ElectricCar(Car):
def __init__(self, brand, model, battery_capacity):
super().__init__(brand, model)
self.battery_capacity = battery_capacity
def charge(self):
```

print(f"Charging {self.brand} {self.model}")

In this example, **ElectricCar** is a subclass of **Car**, inheriting its attributes and methods. The **__init__** method of the superclass is called using **super()** to initialize inherited attributes.

By understanding and applying these OOP concepts in Python, developers can design modular, flexible, and maintainable code. Classes and objects allow for a structured approach to programming, promoting code organization and reuse. Inheritance enables code extension and specialization, facilitating the creation of hierarchies of related classes. Overall, OOP provides a powerful paradigm for building complex software systems in Python.

Implementing Classes and Objects in Python:

In Python, classes serve as blueprints for creating objects, which are instances of those classes. By defining classes and creating objects from them, developers can encapsulate data (attributes) and behavior (methods) into cohesive units, promoting code reusability and modularity. This section explores how to implement classes and objects in Python, focusing on attributes, methods, and constructors.

Attributes:

- Attributes are variables associated with objects, representing their state or properties.
- They store data that describes the characteristics of objects.
- Attributes can be defined within the class using class variables or instance variables.

```
class Car:
# Class attribute
wheels = 4
def __init__(self, brand, model):
# Instance attributes
```

self.brand = brand
self.model = model
Methods:

- Methods are functions associated with objects, representing their behavior or actions.
- They define the operations that objects of the class can perform.
- Methods can be instance methods, class methods, or static methods.

```
class Car:
def __init__(self, brand, model):
self.brand = brand
self.model = model
# Instance method
def drive(self):
print(f"Driving {self.brand} {self.model}")
# Class method
@classmethod
def get_wheels(cls):
return cls.wheels
# Static method
@staticmethod
def honk():
print("Beep beep!")
```

Constructors:

- Constructors are special methods used for initializing objects of a class.
- In Python, the constructor method is named **__init__**, and it is automatically called when an object is created.
- Constructors can accept parameters to initialize object attributes.

```
class Car:
def __init__(self, brand, model):
self.brand = brand
self.model = model
```

Creating Objects:

- Objects are instances of classes, created by calling the class name followed by parentheses.
- Arguments passed to the class constructor are used to initialize object attributes.

```
# Creating objects (instances) of the Car class
car1 = Car("Toyota", "Camry")
car2 = Car("Honda", "Civic")
```

Accessing Attributes and Calling Methods:

- Attributes and methods of objects are accessed using dot notation (**object.attribute** or **object.method()**).

```
# Accessing attributes
print(car1.brand) # Output: Toyota
print(car2.model) # Output: Civic
# Calling methods
car1.drive() # Output: Driving Toyota Camry
Car.honk() # Output: Beep beep!
```

By implementing classes and objects in Python, developers can create structured and modular code that promotes code reuse and maintainability. Attributes represent the state of objects, methods define their behavior, and constructors initialize object attributes. Understanding these concepts enables developers to design and implement effective object-oriented solutions in Python.

The following are more detailed classes:

Attributes:

In Object-Oriented Programming (OOP) with Python, classes and objects are fundamental concepts used to structure and organize code. Attributes, also known as properties or fields, are variables associated with objects, representing their state or characteristics. Understanding how to implement attributes in Python classes is crucial for creating effective object-oriented designs. Let's explore how to define and work with attributes in Python classes:

1. **Defining Attributes**:
   - Attributes are declared within class definitions and are accessed using dot notation (**object.attribute**).
   - They can be instance attributes, class attributes, or special attributes.

```python
class Car:
# Class attribute
wheels = 4
def __init__(self, brand, model):
# Instance attributes
self.brand = brand
self.model = model
```

Instance Attributes:

- Instance attributes belong to individual objects and have unique values for each object.
- They are defined within the **__init__()** method, which serves as the constructor for the class.
- Instance attributes are initialized using the **self** parameter, which refers to the current instance of the class.

```python
class Car:
def __init__(self, brand, model):
self.brand = brand
```

self.model = model

Class Attributes:

- Class attributes are shared among all instances of a class and have the same value for each object.
- They are declared outside of any method within the class body.
- Class attributes are accessed using the class name (**Class.attribute**) or instance objects.

```
class Car:
wheels = 4
def __init__(self, brand, model):
self.brand = brand
self.model = model
```

Accessing Attributes:

- Attributes can be accessed and modified using dot notation (**object.attribute**).
- Instance attributes are accessed through instance objects, while class attributes are accessed through the class itself or instance objects.

```
# Creating an instance of the Car class
car = Car("Toyota", "Camry")
# Accessing instance attributes
print(car.brand) # Output: Toyota
print(car.model) # Output: Camry
# Accessing class attributes
print(Car.wheels) # Output: 4
```

Attribute Visibility:

- In Python, attributes can be public, private, or protected.

- Public attributes are accessible from outside the class, private attributes are accessible only within the class, and protected attributes have limited accessibility.

```python
class Car:
def __init__(self, brand, model):
self.brand = brand # Public attribute
self._model = model # Protected attribute
self.__year = 2022 # Private attribute
```

Attribute Methods:

- Attribute methods, also known as getter and setter methods, are used to access and modify private attributes indirectly.
- Getter methods retrieve the value of an attribute, while setter methods modify the value.

```python
class Car:
def __init__(self, brand, model, year):
self.brand = brand
self.model = model
self.__year = year
def get_year(self):
return self.__year
def set_year(self, year):
self.__year = year
```

Attributes play a crucial role in defining the state and behavior of objects in Python classes. By understanding how to define, access, and manipulate attributes, developers can create well-structured and robust object-oriented designs for their Python programs.

Methods:

In Object-Oriented Programming (OOP) with Python, methods are functions defined within a class that operate on the attributes of objects. Methods encapsulate behavior and functionality associated with objects, allowing for reusable and modular code. Understanding how to implement methods in Python classes is essential for building effective object-oriented designs. Let's explore how to define and work with methods in Python classes:

Defining Methods:

- Methods are defined within class definitions and are called using dot notation (**object.method()**).
- They typically take the **self** parameter as the first argument, which refers to the instance of the class.

```
class Car:
def __init__(self, brand, model):
self.brand = brand
self.model = model
def drive(self):
return f"Driving {self.brand} {self.model}"
```

Instance Methods:

- Instance methods operate on specific instances of a class and can access and modify instance attributes.
- They are defined without the **@staticmethod** or **@classmethod** decorators and take the **self** parameter.

```
class Car:
def __init__(self, brand, model):
self.brand = brand
self.model = model
def drive(self):
return f"Driving {self.brand} {self.model}"
```

Class Methods:

- Class methods operate on the class itself rather than individual instances.

- They are defined using the **@classmethod** decorator and take the **cls** parameter, referring to the class.

```python
class Car:
wheels = 4
@classmethod
def get_wheels(cls):
return cls.wheels
```

Static Methods:

- Static methods are independent of class and instance attributes and don't require the **self** or **cls** parameters.
- They are defined using the **@staticmethod** decorator and are called using the class name.

```python
class Math:
@staticmethod
def add(a, b):
return a + b
```

Special Methods (Magic Methods):

- Special methods provide functionality for specific operations and behaviors, such as object initialization, comparison, and iteration.
- They are identified by double underscores (__) before and after the method name (e.g., __init__, __str__).

```python
class Car:
def __init__(self, brand, model):
self.brand = brand
self.model = model
def __str__(self):
return f"{self.brand} {self.model}"
```

Accessing Methods:

- Methods are accessed using dot notation (**object.method()**).
- Instance methods are called on instance objects, while class methods and static methods are called on the class itself.

```python
# Creating an instance of the Car class
car = Car("Toyota", "Camry")
# Calling instance method
print(car.drive()) # Output: Driving Toyota Camry
# Calling class method
print(Car.get_wheels()) # Output: 4
```

Methods are essential components of Python classes, providing behavior and functionality to objects. By understanding how to define and use methods effectively, developers can create well-structured and versatile object-oriented designs for their Python programs.

Constructors:

In Object-Oriented Programming (OOP) with Python, constructors are special methods used for initializing objects of a class. Constructors ensure that objects are properly initialized with initial values for their attributes. Understanding how to implement constructors in Python classes is crucial for creating well-structured and robust object-oriented designs. Let's explore constructors in Python classes in detail:

What is a Constructor?:

- A constructor is a special method that gets called automatically when an object of a class is created.
- In Python, the constructor method is named **__init__()**, and it is used to initialize object attributes with initial values.
- Constructors ensure that objects are initialized properly before they are used.

```python
class Car:
```

```
def __init__(self, brand, model):
self.brand = brand
self.model = model
```

Initializing Attributes:

- Within the constructor (**__init__()** method), instance attributes are initialized using the **self** parameter.
- The **self** parameter refers to the current instance of the class and allows access to instance attributes and methods.

```
class Car:
def __init__(self, brand, model):
self.brand = brand
self.model = model
```

Parameterized Constructors:

- Constructors in Python can accept parameters, allowing for customization during object initialization.
- Parameters passed to the constructor are used to initialize object attributes with specific values.

```
class Car:
def __init__(self, brand, model, year):
self.brand = brand
self.model = model
self.year = year
```

Default Values:

- Constructor parameters can have default values, allowing objects to be initialized with default attribute values if specific values are not provided during object creation.

```
class Car:
```

```python
def __init__(self, brand="Toyota", model="Camry"):
self.brand = brand
self.model = model
```

Calling the Constructor:

- The constructor is automatically called when an object of the class is created using the class name followed by parentheses.
- Arguments passed to the constructor are used to initialize object attributes.

```python
# Creating objects (instances) of the Car class
car1 = Car("Toyota", "Camry")
car2 = Car("Honda", "Civic")
```

Initializer Method:

- In addition to the constructor, Python also supports an initializer method named **__new__**(), which is responsible for creating new instances of the class.
- The **__new__**() method is rarely used directly, as most object creation is handled by the constructor (**__init__**() method).

```python
class Car:
def __new__(cls, *args, **kwargs):
instance = super().__new__(cls)
return instance
def __init__(self, brand, model):
self.brand = brand
self.model = model
```

Constructors are essential components of Python classes, ensuring that objects are properly initialized with initial attribute values. By understanding how to define and use constructors effectively, developers can create well-structured and maintainable object-oriented designs for their Python programs.

Understanding Inheritance:

Object-Oriented Programming (OOP) in Python encompasses powerful concepts like inheritance, polymorphism, and encapsulation. These concepts enable developers to build modular, extensible, and maintainable code. Let's explore each of these concepts in detail:

Inheritance:

- Inheritance is a mechanism where a new class (subclass) inherits properties and behaviors from an existing class (superclass).
- Subclasses can extend or modify the functionality of the superclass, promoting code reuse and modularity.
- In Python, inheritance is implemented by specifying the name of the superclass in parentheses after the subclass name in the class definition.

```python
# Example of inheritance in Python
class Animal:
def sound(self):
print("Animal sound")
class Dog(Animal):
def sound(self):
print("Bark")
class Cat(Animal):
def sound(self):
print("Meow")
```

Polymorphism:

- Polymorphism allows objects of different classes to be treated as objects of a common superclass.
- It enables methods to behave differently based on the type of object they operate on, enhancing flexibility and modularity.

- In Python, polymorphism is achieved through method overriding, where a subclass provides a specific implementation of a method defined in its superclass.

```
# Example of polymorphism in Python
def make_sound(animal):
animal.sound()
dog = Dog()
cat = Cat()
make_sound(dog) # Output: Bark
make_sound(cat) # Output: Meow
```

Encapsulation:

- Encapsulation is the bundling of data (attributes) and methods (behaviors) that operate on that data within a single unit (class).
- It allows for data hiding, preventing direct access to internal attributes from outside the class.
- Access to attributes and methods is controlled using access specifiers like public, private, and protected.

```
# Example of encapsulation in Python
class BankAccount:
def __init__(self, account_number, balance):
self._account_number = account_number # Protected attribute
self.__balance = balance # Private attribute
def deposit(self, amount):
self.__balance += amount
def withdraw(self, amount):
if amount <= self.__balance:
self.__balance -= amount
else:
print("Insufficient funds")
```

In summary, inheritance allows for code reuse and extension, polymorphism enables flexible and modular code, and encapsulation promotes data hiding and abstraction. By leveraging these OOP concepts in Python, developers can design robust and maintainable software solutions that are scalable and easy to understand. Understanding these principles is essential for proficient Python programming and software development.

Exploring Advanced OOP Topics:

Object-Oriented Programming (OOP) in Python extends beyond basic concepts like classes, objects, inheritance, polymorphism, and encapsulation. Advanced OOP topics such as class decorators, abstract base classes, and metaprogramming provide developers with additional tools and techniques to create flexible, maintainable, and powerful software solutions. Let's delve into each of these advanced topics:

Class Decorators:

- Class decorators are functions that modify or extend the behavior of classes and their methods.
- They are applied using the @ syntax before the class definition.
- Class decorators can be used for various purposes, including adding logging, validation, caching, or other cross-cutting concerns to classes and methods.

```python
# Example of class decorator in Python
def add_logging(cls):
for name, method in vars(cls).items():
if callable(method):
setattr(cls, name, log_method(method))
return cls
def log_method(method):
def wrapper(*args, **kwargs):
print(f"Calling      {method.__name__}      with      args={args},
kwargs={kwargs}")
return method(*args, **kwargs)
```

```
return wrapper
@add_logging
class Calculator:
def add(self, a, b):
return a + b
def subtract(self, a, b):
return a - b
```

Abstract Base Classes (ABCs):

- Abstract Base Classes provide a way to define abstract interfaces for classes.
- They cannot be instantiated directly but can be subclassed to provide concrete implementations.
- ABCs enforce the implementation of certain methods in subclasses, promoting code consistency and reliability.

```
from abc import ABC, abstractmethod
class Shape(ABC):
@abstractmethod
def area(self):
pass
@abstractmethod
def perimeter(self):
pass
class Rectangle(Shape):
def __init__(self, width, height):
self.width = width
self.height = height
def area(self):
return self.width * self.height
def perimeter(self):
return 2 * (self.width + self.height)
```

Metaprogramming:

- Metaprogramming involves writing code that manipulates other parts of the program, such as classes, functions, or modules, at runtime.
- Python's dynamic nature and introspection capabilities make it well-suited for metaprogramming tasks.
- Metaclasses, decorators, and class and function attributes are common tools used in metaprogramming.

```python
# Example of metaclass in Python
class SingletonMeta(type):
_instances = {}
def __call__(cls, *args, **kwargs):
if cls not in cls._instances:
cls._instances[cls] = super().__call__(*args, **kwargs)
return cls._instances[cls]
class Singleton(metaclass=SingletonMeta):
def __init__(self, value):
self.value = value
```

In summary, exploring advanced OOP topics in Python like class decorators, abstract base classes, and metaprogramming empowers developers to write more expressive, maintainable, and powerful code. These concepts provide additional flexibility and control over class and object behavior, enabling the creation of sophisticated software solutions. Understanding and mastering these advanced OOP topics is essential for becoming a proficient Python developer.

12

Chapter 5: File Handling Operations

File handling and input/output (I/O) operations are essential aspects of programming in Python, enabling interaction with external files, streams, and devices. Python provides versatile tools and libraries for reading from and writing to files, as well as handling input and output operations.

Opening and Closing Files:

- Files are opened using the built-in **open()** function, specifying the file path and the mode (e.g., read, write, append).
- It's important to close files after performing operations on them to release system resources using the **close()** method or the context manager (**with** statement).

```python
# Example of opening and closing files in Python
file_path = "example.txt"
# Opening a file for reading
file = open(file_path, "r")
# Perform operations on the file
```

file.close()

Reading from Files:

- Python provides various methods for reading data from files, including **read()**, **readline()**, and **readlines()**.
- The **read()** method reads the entire contents of the file, **readline()** reads a single line, and **readlines()** reads all lines into a list.

```python
# Example of reading from a file in Python
with open(file_path, "r") as file:
content = file.read() # Read entire content
line = file.readline() # Read a single line
lines = file.readlines() # Read all lines into a list
```

Writing to Files:

- To write data to files, Python provides methods like **write()** and **writelines()**.
- The **write()** method writes a string to the file, while **writelines()** writes a list of strings to the file.

```python
# Example of writing to a file in Python
with open(file_path, "w") as file:
file.write("Hello, World!\n")
file.writelines(["Line 1\n", "Line 2\n", "Line 3\n"])
```

File Modes:

- File modes define the purpose and permissions of file operations. Common modes include:
    - **"r"**: Read mode (default), allows reading from the file.
    - **"w"**: Write mode, truncates the file if it exists, creates a new file if it doesn't.

- ○ "**a**": Append mode, appends data to the end of the file.
- ○ "**b**": Binary mode, for handling binary files.
- ○ "**+**": Read/write mode.

Input/Output Operations:

- Python provides built-in functions like **input()** and **print()** for handling input and output operations interactively.
- The **input()** function reads input from the user as a string, while **print()** outputs data to the console.

```python
# Example of input/output operations in Python
name = input("Enter your name: ")
print("Hello, " + name + "!")
```

Standard Streams:

- Python uses standard streams **stdin**, **stdout**, and **stderr** for input, output, and error messages, respectively.
- These streams are accessed using the **sys** module from the standard library.

```python
import sys
# Reading from standard input
data = sys.stdin.readline()
# Writing to standard output
sys.stdout.write("Output data\n")
# Writing to standard error
sys.stderr.write("Error message\n")
```

File handling and I/O operations are fundamental for interacting with data stored in files and performing input/output tasks in Python programs. Understanding these concepts and mastering their usage enables developers to build robust and efficient software solutions that effectively handle data input, output, and processing.

Working With Files and Directories in Python:

File handling is a crucial aspect of programming, allowing developers to interact with external files, read data from them, write data to them, and manipulate their contents. Python provides powerful tools and libraries for performing file operations efficiently.

Opening and Closing Files:

- Before performing any operations on a file, it needs to be opened using the **open()** function.
- The **open()** function takes two arguments: the file path and the mode (e.g., read mode, write mode, append mode).
- After completing file operations, it's important to close the file using the **close()** method to release system resources.

```python
# Opening a file for reading
file = open("example.txt", "r")
# Perform operations on the file
file.close()
```

Reading from Files:

- Python provides various methods for reading data from files, including **read()**, **readline()**, and **readlines()**.
- The **read()** method reads the entire contents of the file as a string, **readline()** reads a single line, and **readlines()** reads all lines into a list.

```python
# Reading from a file
with open("example.txt", "r") as file:
content = file.read() # Read entire content
line = file.readline() # Read a single line
lines = file.readlines() # Read all lines into a list
```

Writing to Files:

- To write data to files, Python provides methods like **write()** and **writelines()**.
- The **write()** method writes a string to the file, while **writelines()** writes a list of strings to the file.

```
# Writing to a file
with open("example.txt", "w") as file:
file.write("Hello, World!\n")
file.writelines(["Line 1\n", "Line 2\n", "Line 3\n"])
```

Manipulating File Contents:

- Python allows for various operations on file contents, such as appending, deleting, or modifying data.
- To append data to a file, open it in append mode ("a") and use the **write()** method.
- To delete a file, use the **os.remove()** function from the **os** module.

```
import os
# Appending data to a file
with open("example.txt", "a") as file:
file.write("Additional data\n")
# Deleting a file
os.remove("example.txt")
```

Working with Directories:

- Python's **os** module provides functions for working with directories, such as creating, removing, and listing directories.
- To create a directory, use the **os.makedirs()** function.
- To remove a directory, use the **os.rmdir()** function.
- To list the contents of a directory, use the **os.listdir()** function.

```python
import os
# Creating a directory
os.makedirs("my_directory")
# Removing a directory
os.rmdir("my_directory")
# Listing contents of a directory
contents = os.listdir("my_directory")
```

Working with files and directories in Python is fundamental for many applications, allowing developers to manage data effectively. By mastering file operations, developers can create robust and efficient software solutions that handle various input/output tasks seamlessly. Understanding these concepts is essential for proficient Python programming and software development.

The Following Are More Detailed Explanations:

Reading:

Reading from files is a common task in Python programming, allowing developers to access and process data stored in external files. Python provides versatile tools and libraries for reading data from files efficiently.

Opening Files for Reading:

- Before reading data from a file, it needs to be opened in read mode using the **open()** function.
- The **open()** function takes the file path and the mode as arguments, with "r" indicating read mode.

```python
# Opening a file for reading
file = open("example.txt", "r")
```

Reading Entire File Contents:

- The **read()** method reads the entire contents of the file as a string.
- This method is useful when the size of the file is relatively small and can fit into memory.

```
# Reading entire file contents
content = file.read()
```

Reading Line by Line:

- For large files or when processing line-based data, it's common to read the file line by line.
- The **readline()** method reads a single line from the file.

```
# Reading file line by line
line = file.readline()
```

Reading All Lines into a List:

- The **readlines()** method reads all lines from the file and stores them in a list.
- Each element of the list represents a line from the file.

```
# Reading all lines into a list
lines = file.readlines()
```

Using Context Managers (with Statement):

- Python's **with** statement is commonly used when working with files to ensure proper resource management.
- When using a **with** statement, the file is automatically closed after exiting the block, even if an exception occurs.

```
# Using with statement for file reading
with open("example.txt", "r") as file:
content = file.read()
```

Handling File Not Found Errors:

- It's important to handle situations where the file being read does not exist.

- Python's **try** and **except** statements can be used to catch **FileNotFoundError** exceptions.

```
try:
file = open("example.txt", "r")
content = file.read()
except FileNotFoundError:
print("File not found.")
```

Unicode Encoding:

- When working with text files that contain non-ASCII characters, it's important to specify the encoding.
- The **open()** function accepts an optional **encoding** parameter to specify the file encoding.

```
with open("example.txt", "r", encoding="utf-8") as file:
content = file.read()
```

Reading from files in Python is a fundamental skill for data processing, text analysis, and various other applications. By mastering file reading techniques, developers can efficiently access and manipulate data stored in external files, enabling the development of powerful and versatile software solutions.

Writing:

Writing to files is an essential task in Python programming, allowing developers to store data generated by their programs for future use or analysis. Python provides powerful tools and libraries for writing data to files efficiently.

Opening Files for Writing:

- Before writing data to a file, it needs to be opened in write mode using the **open()** function.
- The **open()** function takes the file path and the mode as arguments, with "w" indicating write mode.

```python
# Opening a file for writing
file = open("output.txt", "w")
```

Writing Data to Files:

- The **write()** method is used to write data to the file.
- It takes a string as an argument and writes it to the file.

```python
# Writing data to the file
file.write("Hello, World!\n")
```

Writing Multiple Lines to Files:

- To write multiple lines of data to a file, use the **write()** method multiple times or use the **writelines()** method.
- The **writelines()** method takes a list of strings as an argument and writes each string to the file.

```python
# Writing multiple lines to the file
lines = ["Line 1\n", "Line 2\n", "Line 3\n"]
file.writelines(lines)
```

Using Context Managers (with Statement):

- As with reading files, it's recommended to use a **with** statement when writing to files to ensure proper resource management.
- The file is automatically closed after exiting the **with** block.

```python
# Using with statement for file writing
with open("output.txt", "w") as file:
    file.write("Hello, World!\n")
    file.writelines(["Line 1\n", "Line 2\n", "Line 3\n"])
```

Appending Data to Files:

- To append data to an existing file without overwriting its contents, open the file in append mode using "a" as the mode argument.

```
# Appending data to the file
with open("output.txt", "a") as file:
file.write("Additional data\n")
```

Unicode Encoding:

- When working with text data containing non-ASCII characters, it's important to specify the encoding to ensure proper handling of characters.
- The **open()** function accepts an optional **encoding** parameter to specify the file encoding.

```
with open("output.txt", "w", encoding="utf-8") as file:
file.write("Hello, World!\n")
```

Handling Errors:

- It's important to handle errors that may occur during file writing, such as permission errors or disk space issues.
- Python's **try** and **except** statements can be used to catch and handle exceptions gracefully.

```
try:
with open("output.txt", "w") as file:
file.write("Hello, World!\n")
except OSError as e:
print(f"Error writing to file: {e}")
```

Writing to files in Python is essential for various applications, including data storage, logging, and output generation. By mastering file writing techniques, developers can effectively store and manage data generated by their Python programs, enabling the development of robust and efficient software solutions.

Manipulating File Contents:

Manipulating file contents involves various operations such as modifying, appending, deleting, or analyzing data within files. Python offers powerful tools and libraries for performing these operations efficiently.

Opening Files for Manipulation:

- Before manipulating file contents, the file needs to be opened in the appropriate mode using the **open()** function.
- Modes such as read mode ("r"), write mode ("w"), append mode ("a"), or read/write mode ("r+") can be used based on the required operation.

```python
# Opening a file for manipulation
with open("example.txt", "r+") as file:
# Perform manipulation operations here
```

Reading File Contents:

- Before manipulating file contents, it's common to read the existing data from the file.
- The **read()** method reads the entire contents of the file as a string, while **readlines()** reads all lines into a list.

```python
# Reading file contents
with open("example.txt", "r") as file:
content = file.read() # Read entire content
lines = file.readlines() # Read all lines into a list
```

Modifying File Contents:

- After reading the file contents, modifications can be made as required.

- For example, modifying specific lines, replacing text, or applying transformations to the data.

```
# Modifying file contents
with open("example.txt", "r+") as file:
lines = file.readlines()
# Modify specific lines or content here
# Write modified content back to the file
file.seek(0) # Move the file cursor to the beginning
file.writelines(lines) # Write modified lines back to the file
file.truncate() # Truncate the file to remove any remaining content
```

Appending Data to Files:

- To append new data to the existing file contents, open the file in append mode ("a") and use the **write()** method.

```
# Appending data to a file
with open("example.txt", "a") as file:
file.write("New data to append\n")
```

Deleting File Contents:

- If needed, the entire content of a file can be deleted by truncating the file using the **truncate()** method.

```
# Deleting file contents
with open("example.txt", "r+") as file:
file.truncate(0) # Truncate the file to remove all content
```

Analyzing File Contents:

- Python provides various libraries and methods for analyzing file contents, such as counting lines, searching for specific patterns, or extracting data.

```
# Analyzing file contents
with open("example.txt", "r") as file:
lines = file.readlines()
line_count = len(lines)
# Perform additional analysis as needed
```

Renaming and Deleting Files:

- Python's **os** module provides functions for renaming and deleting files, if necessary.

```
import os
# Renaming a file
os.rename("old_name.txt", "new_name.txt")
# Deleting a file
os.remove("example.txt")
```

Manipulating file contents in Python is essential for a wide range of applications, including data processing, text manipulation, and file management tasks. By mastering file manipulation techniques, developers can effectively modify and manage data stored in files, enabling the development of robust and efficient software solutions.

Understanding File Modes:

File modes in Python specify how files should be opened and interacted with. They dictate whether the file can be read from, written to, or both, as well as other behaviors such as appending data to existing files or creating new files if they don't exist. Understanding file modes is crucial for performing various input/output operations in Python. Let's explore the different file modes available:

Read Mode ("r"):

- Opens the file for reading only.
- If the file doesn't exist, it raises a **FileNotFoundError**.

- The file pointer is placed at the beginning of the file.

file = open("example.txt", "r")
Write Mode ("w"):

- Opens the file for writing only.
- If the file exists, its contents are overwritten. If it doesn't exist, a new file is created.
- The file pointer is placed at the beginning of the file.

file = open("example.txt", "w")
Append Mode ("a"):

- Opens the file for writing only.
- If the file exists, new data is appended to the end of the file. If it doesn't exist, a new file is created.
- The file pointer is placed at the end of the file.

file = open("example.txt", "a")
Read and Write Mode ("r+"):

- Opens the file for both reading and writing.
- The file pointer is placed at the beginning of the file.
- If the file doesn't exist, it raises a **FileNotFoundError**.

file = open("example.txt", "r+")
Write and Read Mode ("w+"):

- Opens the file for both reading and writing.
- If the file exists, its contents are overwritten. If it doesn't exist, a new file is created.
- The file pointer is placed at the beginning of the file.

file = open("example.txt", "a+")

Binary Mode ("b"):

- Used in conjunction with other modes to open files in binary mode, allowing for binary data manipulation.
- For example, "rb" for reading binary, "wb" for writing binary, "ab" for appending binary.

file = open("example.bin", "rb")

Remember to close files after using them to release system resources:

file.close()

Alternatively, use a **with** statement to automatically close the file when the block is exited:

with open("example.txt", "r") as file:

Perform file operations here

Understanding file modes in Python empowers developers to effectively manage file operations, enabling the creation, reading, writing, and manipulation of files in Python programs.

Understanding File Pointers:

File pointers are essential components of file handling in Python. They represent the current position within a file where the next read or write operation will occur. Understanding file pointers is crucial for navigating, reading, and writing data within files accurately. Let's delve into the details of file pointers in Python:

File Pointer Basics:

- Every open file in Python has an associated file pointer.
- The file pointer indicates the position within the file where the next read or write operation will take place.
- Initially, the file pointer is positioned at the beginning of the file (offset 0) when the file is opened.

Navigating the File Pointer:

- Python provides methods to move the file pointer to different positions within the file:
  - **seek(offset, whence)**: Moves the file pointer to the specified position.
    - **offset**: The number of bytes to move the pointer.
    - **whence**: Optional parameter indicating the reference point for the offset.
      - 0: Start of the file (default).
      - 1: Current position.
      - 2: End of the file.

After a seek operation, subsequent read or write operations will occur from the new file pointer position.

```
# Move file pointer to the 10th byte from the start of the file
file.seek(10)
# Move file pointer to the beginning of the file
file.seek(0, 0)
```

Getting the Current File Pointer Position:

- The **tell()** method returns the current position of the file pointer within the file.

```
position = file.tell() # Get current file pointer position
```

Reading and Writing with File Pointers:

- When reading from a file, the file pointer advances automatically as data is read.
- Similarly, when writing to a file, the file pointer advances as data is written.

```
# Reading data from a file
data = file.read(100) # Reads 100 bytes
```

Seeking and Appending:

- When opening a file in append mode ("a"), the file pointer is initially positioned at the end of the file.
- This allows for appending data directly to the end of the file without overwriting existing content.

```
# Opening a file in append mode
with open("example.txt", "a") as file:
# File pointer is at the end of the file
file.write("New data appended\n") # Append data to the end of
the file
```

Understanding file pointers enables developers to precisely control the position within a file when performing read and write operations. By leveraging file pointers effectively, developers can navigate and manipulate file contents with accuracy and efficiency, facilitating various input/output operations in Python programs.

Understanding File Management Techniques:

File management techniques encompass various strategies and practices for efficiently handling files and directories in Python. These techniques enable developers to create, open, read, write, manipulate, and delete files and directories effectively. Let's explore some fundamental file management techniques in Python:

File Creation and Opening:

- Use the **open()** function to create and open files in different modes (read, write, append, read/write).
- Specify the file path and the desired mode as arguments to the **open()** function.

```
file = open("example.txt", "w") # Create/open a file in write mode
```

Closing Files:

- Always close files after performing operations to release system resources and avoid potential issues.

- Use the **close()** method to close the file object.

```
file.close() # Close the file
```

Context Managers (with Statement):

- Utilize the **with** statement as a context manager for file operations to ensure files are automatically closed after use.
- This prevents resource leaks and ensures proper file management.

```
with open("example.txt", "r") as file:
# Perform file operations within the context
```

Reading and Writing Data:

- Use various methods such as **read()**, **readline()**, **readlines()** for reading data from files.
- Use **write()** or **writelines()** for writing data to files.

```
# Reading data from a file
content = file.read()
# Writing data to a file
file.write("Hello, World!\n")
```

Manipulating File Contents:

- After reading file contents, manipulate them as needed (e.g., modify, append, delete).
- Use file pointer manipulation (**seek()**) to navigate within the file.

```
# Appending data to a file
with open("example.txt", "a") as file:
file.write("Additional data\n")
```

Directory Operations:

- Use the **os** module for directory-related operations such as creating, listing, renaming, and deleting directories.

```
import os
# Creating a directory
os.makedirs("my_directory")
# Listing contents of a directory
contents = os.listdir("my_directory")
```

Error Handling:

- Implement error handling to gracefully handle exceptions that may occur during file operations (e.g., FileNotFoundError, PermissionError).

```
try:
file = open("example.txt", "r")
# Perform file operations here
except FileNotFoundError:
print("File not found.")
```

Unicode Encoding:

- Specify the encoding parameter when opening files to handle text data containing non-ASCII characters.

```
with open("example.txt", "r", encoding="utf-8") as file:
# Perform file operations with UTF-8 encoding
```

By employing these file management techniques, developers can effectively handle files and directories in Python, ensuring proper data manipulation, resource management, and error handling. These practices contribute to the development of robust and efficient file handling solutions in Python applications.

Interacting with external files:

Python's **subprocess** module provides a powerful way to interact with external files, programs, and processes directly from within a Python script. It enables you to execute system commands, launch external programs, and interact with their input/output streams. When it comes to interacting with external files, the **subprocess** module can be particularly useful for tasks such as copying, moving, deleting files, or executing commands that manipulate files. Let's explore how to leverage the **subprocess** module for interacting with external files:

Executing Shell Commands:

- Use the **subprocess.run()** function to execute shell commands.
- Specify the command as a list of strings, where the first element is the command and subsequent elements are arguments.

```
import subprocess
# Example: Copy a file using the 'cp' command (Unix-like systems)
subprocess.run(["cp", "source_file.txt", "destination_file.txt"])
```

Capturing Output:

- By default, **subprocess.run()** does not capture the output of the command.
- To capture the output, set the **capture_output** parameter to **True**, and access the output using the **stdout** attribute of the returned **CompletedProcess** object.

```
result = subprocess.run(["ls"], capture_output=True, text=True)
print(result.stdout) # Output of the 'ls' command
```

Working Directory:

- Specify the working directory for the subprocess using the **cwd** parameter.

- This allows you to execute commands relative to a specific directory.

```
subprocess.run(["ls"], cwd="/path/to/directory")
```
Error Handling:

- Check the return code of the subprocess to determine if the command executed successfully.
- By default, **subprocess.run()** raises a **CalledProcessError** if the return code is non-zero.

```
try:
subprocess.run(["ls", "non_existent_file.txt"], check=True)
except subprocess.CalledProcessError as e:
print("Error:", e)
```
File I/O Redirection:

- Redirect input/output streams using shell redirection symbols (<, >, |) to interact with files.
- Note that shell redirection might not work on all platforms or with all shell commands.

```
# Example: Redirect output of 'ls' command to a file
subprocess.run(["ls", "-l"], stdout=open("file_listing.txt", "w"))
```
Using Shell=True:

- By default, **subprocess.run()** does not use the shell to execute commands.
- Set **shell=True** to use the shell, allowing you to use shell features like shell expansion, pipes, and redirection.

```
subprocess.run("ls -l | grep .txt", shell=True)
```
Advanced Usage:

- For more complex interactions with external files or programs, use other functions in the **subprocess** module such as **subprocess.Popen()** or **subprocess.call()**.
- These functions offer more control over the subprocess, including handling input/output streams and interacting with the process while it's running.

```
process = subprocess.Popen(["ls"], stdout=subprocess.PIPE)
output, _ = process.communicate()
```

The **subprocess** module in Python provides a flexible and robust way to interact with external files and programs. By understanding its capabilities and best practices, you can efficiently perform various file management tasks and execute system commands directly from your Python scripts, enhancing the versatility and functionality of your applications.

Interacting With External Processes:

Python's **subprocess** module provides a powerful way to interact with external processes, including executing system commands, launching external programs, and communicating with them via input/output streams. This capability is invaluable for performing a wide range of tasks, from simple file operations to complex system administration tasks. Let's delve into how to effectively interact with external processes using the **subprocess** module:

Executing External Commands:

- Use the **subprocess.run()** function to execute external commands.
- Specify the command as a list of strings, where the first element is the command and subsequent elements are arguments.

```
import subprocess
# Example: Execute the 'ls' command
subprocess.run(["ls", "-l"])
```

Capturing Output:

- By default, **subprocess.run()** does not capture the output of the command.
- To capture the output, set the **capture_output** parameter to **True**, and access the output using the **stdout** attribute of the returned **CompletedProcess** object.

```
result = subprocess.run(["ls"], capture_output=True, text=True)
print(result.stdout) # Output of the 'ls' command
```

Handling Errors:

- Check the return code of the subprocess to determine if the command executed successfully.
- By default, **subprocess.run()** raises a **CalledProcessError** if the return code is non-zero.

```
try:
subprocess.run(["ls", "non_existent_file.txt"], check=True)
except subprocess.CalledProcessError as e:
print("Error:", e)
```

Shell Commands and Shell=True:

- By default, **subprocess.run()** does not use the shell to execute commands.
- To use shell features like shell expansion, pipes, and redirection, set **shell=True**.
- Be cautious when using **shell=True** as it may introduce security risks if user input is involved.

```
subprocess.run("ls -l | grep .txt", shell=True)
```

Input to External Commands:

- Pass input to external commands via the **input** parameter.
- If the **input** parameter is specified, the command's stdin stream is redirected from the given input.

```
subprocess.run(["grep", "pattern"], input=b"input_data", text=True)
```

Piping Output:

- Use the **stdout** parameter to redirect the standard output of one command to the standard input of another command, creating a pipeline.
- This allows you to chain multiple commands together.

```
result = subprocess.run(["ls", "-l"], stdout=subprocess.PIPE, text=True)
subprocess.run(["grep", ".txt"], input=result.stdout, text=True)
```

Advanced Usage:

- For more complex interactions with external processes, use other functions in the **subprocess** module such as **subprocess.Popen()** or **subprocess.call()**.
- These functions offer more control over the subprocess, including handling input/output streams and interacting with the process while it's running.

```
process = subprocess.Popen(["ls"], stdout=subprocess.PIPE)
output, _ = process.communicate()
```

By leveraging the **subprocess** module, you can seamlessly integrate external commands and programs into your Python scripts, enabling automation, system administration, and a wide range of other tasks. With proper error handling and security considerations, **subprocess** provides a robust and flexible solution for interacting with external processes in Python.

Handling Exceptions:

When working with files in Python, it's essential to handle exceptions gracefully to ensure your program behaves predictably, especially in scenarios where file-related operations may fail due to various reasons such as file not found, permission denied, or invalid file format. Proper exception handling can prevent unexpected crashes and provide informative error messages to users. Here's a comprehensive guide on handling exceptions in file operations:

Opening Files:

- When opening files using the **open()** function, wrap it in a **try-except** block to catch any potential exceptions.

```
try:
file = open("example.txt", "r")
except FileNotFoundError:
print("File not found.")
except PermissionError:
print("Permission denied.")
except Exception as e:
print("Error:", e)
```

Reading from Files:

- Handle exceptions that may occur while reading from files, such as **IOError** or **UnicodeDecodeError**.

```
try:
with open("example.txt", "r") as file:
content = file.read()
except IOError:
print("Error reading file.")
except UnicodeDecodeError:
print("Error decoding file contents.")
```

Writing to Files:

- Catch exceptions that may occur during writing operations, such as **IOError** or **PermissionError**.

```
try:
with open("output.txt", "w") as file:
file.write("Some data to write")
except IOError:
print("Error writing to file.")
except PermissionError:
print("Permission denied.")
```

Closing Files:

- Although using a **with** statement automatically closes files, you can still catch exceptions that may occur during the closing operation.

```
try:
with open("example.txt", "r") as file:
# Perform file operations
pass
except Exception as e:
print("Error:", e)
finally:
try:
file.close()
except AttributeError:
pass # File wasn't opened successfully
```

Handling Multiple Exceptions:

- You can handle multiple exceptions in a single **except** block, or have separate **except** blocks for different types of exceptions.

```python
try:
with open("example.txt", "r") as file:
content = file.read()
except (FileNotFoundError, PermissionError):
print("File not found or permission denied.")
except Exception as e:
print("Error:", e)
```

Custom Error Messages:

- Provide informative error messages to users or log detailed error information for debugging purposes.

```python
try:
file = open("example.txt", "r")
except FileNotFoundError:
print("Error: File 'example.txt' not found.")
except PermissionError:
print("Error: Permission denied to open 'example.txt'.")
except Exception as e:
print("An unexpected error occurred:", e)
```

Logging Exceptions:

- Utilize the **logging** module to log exceptions to a file or stream for debugging and error tracking.

```python
import logging
try:
file = open("example.txt", "r")
except FileNotFoundError:
logging.error("File 'example.txt' not found.")
except PermissionError:
logging.error("Permission denied to open 'example.txt'.")
except Exception as e:
```

logging.error("An unexpected error occurred: %s", e)

By properly handling exceptions in file operations, you can ensure that your Python programs handle errors gracefully, provide meaningful feedback to users, and maintain robustness in various file-related scenarios. Effective exception handling is crucial for writing robust and reliable file processing applications.

Handling Errors:

Error handling in file operations is crucial for writing robust and reliable Python programs, especially when dealing with external files where various issues may arise, such as missing files, permission errors, or invalid file formats. Properly handling errors ensures that your program gracefully handles exceptional situations, provides meaningful error messages to users, and avoids unexpected crashes. Here's a comprehensive guide on handling errors in file operations:

Opening Files:

- Handle exceptions that may occur when opening files, such as **FileNotFoundError** or **PermissionError**.

```
try:
file = open("example.txt", "r")
except FileNotFoundError:
print("Error: File not found.")
except PermissionError:
print("Error: Permission denied.")
except Exception as e:
print("An unexpected error occurred:", e)
```

Reading from Files:

- Catch exceptions that may occur during reading operations, such as **IOError**, **UnicodeDecodeError**, or **ValueError**.

```
try:
```

```python
with open("example.txt", "r") as file:
content = file.read()
except IOError:
print("Error: Unable to read file.")
except UnicodeDecodeError:
print("Error: Unable to decode file contents.")
except ValueError:
print("Error: Invalid data encountered while reading.")
```

Writing to Files:

- Handle exceptions that may occur during writing operations, such as **IOError**, **PermissionError**, or **TypeError**.

```python
try:
with open("output.txt", "w") as file:
file.write("Some data to write")
except IOError:
print("Error: Unable to write to file.")
except PermissionError:
print("Error: Permission denied.")
except TypeError:
print("Error: Invalid data type for writing.")
```

Closing Files:

- Although using a **with** statement automatically closes files, handle exceptions that may occur during the closing operation.

```python
try:
with open("example.txt", "r") as file:
# Perform file operations
pass
except Exception as e:
print("An unexpected error occurred:", e)
```

```
finally:
try:
file.close()
except AttributeError:
pass # File wasn't opened successfully
```

Handling Multiple Exceptions:

- You can handle multiple exceptions in a single **except** block or have separate **except** blocks for different types of exceptions.

```
try:
with open("example.txt", "r") as file:
content = file.read()
except (FileNotFoundError, PermissionError):
print("Error: File not found or permission denied.")
except Exception as e:
print("An unexpected error occurred:", e)
```

Custom Error Messages:

- Provide informative error messages to users or log detailed error information for debugging purposes.

```
try:
file = open("example.txt", "r")
except FileNotFoundError:
print("Error: File 'example.txt' not found.")
except PermissionError:
print("Error: Permission denied to open 'example.txt'.")
except Exception as e:
print("An unexpected error occurred:", e)
```

Logging Exceptions:

- Utilize the **logging** module to log exceptions to a file or stream for debugging and error tracking.

```
import logging
try:
file = open("example.txt", "r")
except FileNotFoundError:
logging.error("File 'example.txt' not found.")
except PermissionError:
logging.error("Permission denied to open 'example.txt'.")
except Exception as e:
logging.error("An unexpected error occurred: %s", e)
```

By handling errors effectively in file operations, you can ensure that your Python programs are robust, reliable, and resilient to unexpected issues that may arise when working with external files. Proper error handling enhances the user experience and contributes to the overall quality and stability of your software applications.

13

Chapter 6: Python Standard Library and Modules

The Python Standard Library is a vast collection of modules and packages that provides a wide range of functionalities to accomplish various tasks without the need for external libraries. These modules cover areas such as file I/O, data manipulation, networking, web development, GUI programming, and more. Understanding the Python Standard Library is essential for every Python developer as it offers a wealth of tools and utilities to streamline development tasks. Let's explore the key aspects of the Python Standard Library and its modules:

1. **Built-in Functions and Types**:
   - The Python Standard Library includes built-in functions and types such as **print()**, **len()**, **range()**, **str**, **list**, **dict**, and **tuple**, providing fundamental functionalities for common programming tasks.
2. **File and Directory Access**:

- Modules like **os**, **os.path**, and **shutil** offer functionalities for file and directory operations, including file manipulation, path handling, directory traversal, and file copying.

3. **Data Serialization**:
   - The **json** and **pickle** modules facilitate data serialization and deserialization, allowing data to be stored in a platform-independent format or transferred between different systems.

4. **Data Compression and Archiving**:
   - Modules like **zipfile**, **gzip**, and **tarfile** enable compression and decompression of files, as well as creation and extraction of archive files in various formats.

5. **Concurrency and Parallelism**:
   - The **threading** and **multiprocessing** modules provide support for concurrent and parallel execution of tasks, allowing developers to leverage multiple CPU cores and threads for improved performance.

6. **Networking and Internet Protocols**:
   - Modules such as **socket**, **urllib**, **http**, and **ftplib** offer functionalities for network communication, HTTP requests, FTP operations, and more, enabling interaction with web services and servers.

7. **Database Access**:
   - The **sqlite3** module allows interaction with SQLite databases, offering functionalities for executing SQL queries, managing transactions, and working with database connections.

8. **Regular Expressions**:
   - The **re** module provides support for regular expressions, allowing developers to search, match, and manipulate text using complex pattern-matching rules.

9. **Date and Time Manipulation**:

- The **datetime** module offers functionalities for working with dates, times, time zones, and timedelta objects, facilitating date and time calculations and formatting.

10. **Mathematics and Numeric Processing**:
    - Modules like **math** and **random** provide mathematical functions and utilities for numerical computations, random number generation, and statistical analysis.

11. **Testing and Debugging**:
    - The **unittest** and **doctest** modules support unit testing and test-driven development, while the **pdb** module offers a built-in debugger for debugging Python code interactively.

12. **GUI Development**:
    - Modules such as **tkinter**, **PyQt**, and **wxPython** enable the development of graphical user interfaces (GUIs) for desktop applications, offering widgets, event handling, and layout management.

13. **Data Processing and Analysis**:
    - Modules like **csv**, **json**, **xml**, and **collections** provide functionalities for processing structured data formats, parsing XML documents, and working with specialized data structures.

14. **System Administration and Scripting**:
    - Modules like **subprocess**, **sys**, and **argparse** facilitate system administration tasks, command-line scripting, and interaction with the operating system.

15. **Internationalization and Localization**:
    - The **locale** and **gettext** modules support internationalization and localization of Python applications, allowing for the translation of text and formatting of data based on locale settings.

16. **Security and Cryptography**:

- Modules like **hashlib** and **hmac** offer cryptographic functionalities for secure hashing, message authentication, and encryption, ensuring data integrity and confidentiality.

The Python Standard Library provides a rich ecosystem of modules and packages that empower Python developers to build robust, scalable, and feature-rich applications across a wide range of domains. By leveraging the functionalities offered by the Standard Library, developers can streamline development, reduce dependencies on external libraries, and create efficient and maintainable code. Understanding and mastering the Python Standard Library is essential for becoming a proficient Python developer.

Exploring The Python Standard Library:

The Python Standard Library is an extensive collection of modules and packages that come bundled with every Python installation. These modules provide a wide range of functionalities to facilitate various programming tasks, from basic file operations to advanced networking and web development. Understanding the commonly used modules and their functionalities is essential for every Python developer. Let's explore some of the key modules in the Python Standard Library:

1. **os and os.path**:
    - The **os** module provides a platform-independent interface to operating system functionality, including file and directory operations, process management, and environment variables.
    - The **os.path** module offers functions for path manipulation, such as joining and splitting paths, checking file existence, and getting file information.
2. **sys**:

- The **sys** module provides access to Python interpreter variables and functions, allowing interaction with the Python runtime environment.
- It's commonly used for accessing command-line arguments, managing Python paths, and interacting with the standard input/output streams.

3. **datetime**:

- The **datetime** module offers functionalities for working with dates, times, time zones, and timedelta objects.
- It provides classes like **datetime**, **date**, **time**, and **timedelta** for performing date and time calculations, formatting, and parsing.

4. **json and pickle**:

- The **json** module facilitates JSON serialization and deserialization, allowing data to be represented in a platform-independent format.
- The **pickle** module provides serialization and deserialization of Python objects, allowing objects to be stored and retrieved from files or transmitted over networks.

5. **collections**:

- The **collections** module offers specialized data structures beyond the built-in types, such as **deque**, **Counter**, **defaultdict**, and **namedtuple**.
- These data structures provide enhanced functionalities for tasks like counting elements, creating dictionaries with default values, and representing objects with named fields.

6. **re**:

- The **re** module provides support for regular expressions, allowing developers to search, match, and manipulate text using complex pattern-matching rules.
- It offers functions like **re.search()**, **re.match()**, and **re.sub()** for pattern matching and substitution operations.

7. **math and random**:
   - The **math** module offers mathematical functions and constants for numerical computations, including trigonometric functions, logarithms, and mathematical constants like π and e.
   - The **random** module provides functions for generating random numbers, choosing random elements from sequences, and shuffling sequences.

8. **subprocess**:
   - The **subprocess** module enables the creation of subprocesses and communication with them, allowing execution of external commands and programs from within Python scripts.
   - It offers functions like **subprocess.run()**, **subprocess.Popen()**, and **subprocess.call()** for running commands and managing subprocesses.

9. **logging**:
   - The **logging** module provides a flexible logging framework for Python applications, allowing developers to log messages to various destinations like files, streams, or the console.
   - It supports different logging levels, formatting options, and customizable loggers and handlers.

10. **socket**:
   - The **socket** module offers low-level networking functionalities for communication over sockets, including TCP/IP and UDP protocols.
   - It enables the creation of network clients and servers, handling network connections, and sending/receiving data over networks.

11. **argparse**:

- The **argparse** module provides a powerful and flexible mechanism for parsing command-line arguments and options.
- It simplifies the process of creating command-line interfaces for Python scripts, allowing developers to define arguments, options, and usage messages.

12. **unittest**:

- The **unittest** module supports unit testing in Python, providing a framework for organizing and running test cases and test suites.
- It allows developers to write test cases, assert expected behaviors, and automate the execution of tests to ensure code quality and reliability.

13. **csv and io**:

- The **csv** module offers functionalities for reading and writing CSV (Comma-Separated Values) files, providing easy handling of tabular data.
- The **io** module provides classes and functions for handling input/output operations, including file-like objects, byte streams, and string streams.

14. **urllib**:

- The **urllib** module offers functionalities for making HTTP requests, interacting with web servers, and handling URLs.
- It includes submodules like **urllib.request**, **urllib.parse**, and **urllib.error** for different aspects of URL handling and web interactions.

15. **multiprocessing**:

- The **multiprocessing** module provides support for parallel and concurrent execution of tasks using multiple processes.

○ It offers an API similar to the **threading** module but uses processes instead of threads, avoiding the limitations of the Global Interpreter Lock (GIL).

These are just a few examples of the many modules available in the Python Standard Library. Exploring and familiarizing yourself with these modules and their functionalities will greatly enhance your productivity as a Python developer and enable you to tackle a wide range of programming tasks efficiently and effectively.

Using Third-Party Libraries and Modules:

While the Python Standard Library offers a wide range of functionalities for various programming tasks, developers often find themselves needing additional tools and functionalities that aren't included in the Standard Library. This is where third-party libraries and modules come into play. Third-party libraries are packages developed by the Python community and other organizations to extend Python's capabilities beyond what's available in the Standard Library. Let's explore how developers can leverage third-party libraries to enhance their Python projects:

1. **Rich Ecosystem**: The Python ecosystem boasts a rich repository of third-party libraries covering almost every imaginable domain, from web development and data analysis to machine learning and artificial intelligence. These libraries are developed and maintained by the community and are freely available for anyone to use.

2. **Installation**: Installing third-party libraries in Python is straightforward using package managers like pip (Python's package installer). Developers can simply use the **pip install** command followed by the name of the library to install it. For example, **pip**

install requests installs the popular requests library for making HTTP requests.

3. **Documentation and Community Support**: Most third-party libraries come with comprehensive documentation that explains their functionalities, usage, and API. Additionally, these libraries often have active communities where developers can seek help, ask questions, and contribute to the development of the library.

4. **Specialized Functionalities**: Third-party libraries often specialize in specific areas, providing advanced functionalities and tools tailored to particular domains. For example:
   - **numpy** and **pandas** for numerical and data analysis.
   - **matplotlib** and **seaborn** for data visualization.
   - **Django** and **Flask** for web development.
   - **TensorFlow** and **PyTorch** for machine learning and deep learning.

5. **Code Reusability**: Third-party libraries promote code reusability by providing pre-built solutions to common problems and tasks. Instead of reinventing the wheel, developers can leverage existing libraries to save time and effort in development.

6. **Integration with Existing Code**: Third-party libraries can seamlessly integrate with existing Python codebases, allowing developers to extend the functionality of their applications without having to rewrite everything from scratch.

7. **Open-Source and Customization**: Many third-party libraries are open-source, allowing developers to inspect and modify the source code according to their requirements. This level of customization empowers developers to tailor the libraries to suit their specific needs.

8. **Cross-Platform Compatibility**: Most third-party libraries are designed to be cross-platform, meaning they work seamlessly on different operating systems without requiring any modifications. This ensures that Python applications built using third-party libraries are portable and can run on various platforms.

9. **Continuous Development and Improvement**: Third-party libraries are often actively maintained and updated by their respective communities. This ensures that the libraries stay up-to-date with the latest Python versions, bug fixes, and feature enhancements.

10. **Commercial Support**: Some third-party libraries offer commercial support and services, providing enterprises with additional assistance, training, and consulting to integrate the libraries into their projects effectively.

In summary, third-party libraries play a crucial role in extending Python's capabilities and empowering developers to build diverse and feature-rich applications. By leveraging the vast ecosystem of third-party libraries, Python developers can accelerate development, solve complex problems, and unlock new possibilities in their projects.

Working With Modules for Data Manipulation:

Data manipulation is a fundamental aspect of many Python projects, especially those involving data analysis, processing, and transformation. The Python Standard Library offers several modules that provide powerful tools for working with data efficiently. Let's explore some of these modules and how they can be used for data manipulation:

1. **csv**:
    - The **csv** module allows reading and writing data in CSV (Comma-Separated Values) format, which is a common data interchange format for tabular data.
    - It provides functions for reading CSV files (**csv.reader()**), writing CSV files (**csv.writer()**), and manipulating CSV data rows and columns.
2. **json**:

- The **json** module facilitates the encoding and decoding of JSON (JavaScript Object Notation) data, which is widely used for data interchange on the web and in APIs.
- It offers functions like **json.dumps()** to serialize Python objects into JSON strings, and **json.loads()** to deserialize JSON strings into Python objects.

3. **pickle:**

- The **pickle** module provides functions for serializing and deserializing Python objects, allowing objects to be saved to files or transmitted over networks.
- It supports the serialization of a wide range of Python objects, including custom classes and instances.

4. **shelve:**

- The **shelve** module provides a persistent dictionary-like object that can be used to store and retrieve Python objects from a disk-based database.
- It offers functionalities similar to dictionaries (**shelve.open()**, **shelve.close()**, etc.) for storing and accessing data.

5. **sqlite3:**

- The **sqlite3** module enables interaction with SQLite databases, which are lightweight, self-contained databases that are integrated into Python.
- It provides functions for executing SQL queries (**sqlite3.execute()**), managing database connections (**sqlite3.connect()**), and handling transactions.

6. **collections:**

- The **collections** module offers specialized data structures like **defaultdict**, **Counter**, and **deque** that can be useful for data manipulation tasks.

- For example, **Counter** can be used to count the occurrences of elements in a collection, while **deque** provides efficient insertion and deletion from both ends of a sequence.

7. **itertools**:
   - The **itertools** module provides functions for creating iterators for efficient looping and data manipulation.
   - It offers functions like **itertools.chain()** for chaining together multiple iterators, **itertools.combinations()** for generating combinations of elements, and **itertools.groupby()** for grouping data based on a key function.

8. **decimal**:
   - The **decimal** module provides support for decimal floating-point arithmetic, which is useful for applications requiring precise numerical calculations.
   - It offers the **Decimal** class for representing and performing arithmetic operations on decimal numbers with user-defined precision.

9. **numpy** and **pandas** (third-party libraries):
   - While not part of the Python Standard Library, numpy and pandas are widely used third-party libraries for data manipulation and analysis.
   - numpy provides efficient array operations and mathematical functions, while pandas offers data structures like **DataFrame** and **Series** for handling structured data.

10. **datetime** and **time**:
    - The **datetime** and **time** modules provide functionalities for working with dates, times, and timestamps, which are often encountered in data manipulation tasks.
    - They offer functions for creating, formatting, and manipulating dates and times, as well as for calculating time differences and performing time-related operations.

These modules, along with third-party libraries like numpy and pandas, provide powerful tools for data manipulation in Python. By leveraging these modules effectively, developers can perform a wide range of data processing and transformation tasks efficiently and accurately.

Working With Modules for Web Scraping:

Web scraping is the process of extracting data from websites, and it's a common task in many Python projects, especially those involving data collection, analysis, and automation. The Python Standard Library offers several modules that provide powerful tools for web scraping. Let's explore some of these modules and how they can be used for web scraping:

1. **urllib.request**:
    - The **urllib.request** module allows fetching data from URLs (Uniform Resource Locators) using HTTP protocol.
    - It provides functions like **urlopen()** to open URLs and **read()** to read the content of the response.
2. **requests** (third-party library):
    - While not part of the Python Standard Library, the **requests** library is widely used for making HTTP requests in a more user-friendly and efficient manner compared to **urllib**.
    - It offers functions like **get()** and **post()** for sending HTTP GET and POST requests, and provides features like session management, authentication, and response handling.
3. **beautifulsoup4** (third-party library):
    - The **beautifulsoup4** library is a popular choice for parsing HTML and XML documents, making it easy to extract data from web pages.

- It provides functions for parsing HTML content, navigating the document tree, and searching for specific elements using CSS selectors or XPath expressions.

4. **lxml** (third-party library):
   - **lxml** is another powerful library for parsing XML and HTML documents, offering high-performance and feature-rich functionalities.
   - It provides the **lxml.html** module for parsing HTML content, and the **lxml.etree** module for processing XML documents with an ElementTree-like API.

5. **re**:
   - The **re** module for regular expressions can be used to extract data from web pages based on specific patterns or regular expressions.
   - It allows searching for patterns in strings, extracting matches, and performing complex text processing operations.

6. **html.parser**:
   - The **html.parser** module provides a simple HTML parser as part of the Python Standard Library.
   - While not as feature-rich as **beautifulsoup4** or **lxml**, it can still be used for basic HTML parsing tasks.

7. **robotsparser**:
   - The **robotsparser** module allows parsing and interpreting the **robots.txt** file of a website, which specifies rules for web crawlers and bots.
   - It can be used to determine which URLs can be crawled and which should be avoided.

8. **selenium** (third-party library):
   - **selenium** is a powerful tool for automating web browsers, making it suitable for scraping dynamic websites that rely heavily on JavaScript.

- It allows controlling web browsers programmatically, interacting with web elements, and executing JavaScript code within the browser.

9. **csv** and **json**:
- After scraping data from websites, the **csv** and **json** modules can be used to store the extracted data in CSV or JSON format, respectively.
- They provide functions for writing data to files in the desired format, making it easy to save and process the scraped data.

These modules, along with third-party libraries like **requests**, **beautifulsoup4**, and **selenium**, provide powerful tools for web scraping in Python. By leveraging these modules effectively, developers can extract data from websites efficiently and accurately for a wide range of applications. However, it's essential to respect the website's terms of service and legal requirements while scraping data to avoid potential legal issues.

Working With Modules for Data Visualization:

Data visualization is essential for gaining insights from data and effectively communicating findings to stakeholders. The Python Standard Library, along with third-party libraries, offers several modules for creating various types of visualizations. Let's explore some of these modules and how they can be used for data visualization:

1. **matplotlib**:
- **matplotlib** is one of the most widely used libraries for creating static, interactive, and animated visualizations in Python.
- It provides a MATLAB-like interface for creating plots and charts, including line plots, scatter plots, bar plots, histograms, pie charts, and more.

- **matplotlib** offers extensive customization options for controlling plot appearance, such as colors, markers, labels, titles, and annotations.

2. **seaborn** (third-party library):
   - **seaborn** is built on top of **matplotlib** and provides a higher-level interface for creating statistical visualizations.
   - It offers functions for creating complex statistical plots, such as scatter plots with regression lines, box plots, violin plots, pair plots, and heatmaps.
   - **seaborn** simplifies the process of creating aesthetically pleasing and informative visualizations by automatically handling details like color palettes and data aggregation.

3. **plotly** (third-party library):
   - **plotly** is a versatile library for creating interactive and web-based visualizations in Python.
   - It supports various types of plots, including line plots, scatter plots, bar plots, histograms, box plots, 3D plots, and choropleth maps.
   - **plotly** generates interactive plots that can be embedded in web applications or displayed in Jupyter notebooks, allowing users to explore data dynamically.

4. **bokeh** (third-party library):
   - **bokeh** is another library for creating interactive visualizations in Python, particularly well-suited for creating interactive dashboards and web applications.
   - It offers a high-level interface for creating interactive plots with features like tooltips, zooming, panning, and linked brushing.
   - **bokeh** generates HTML and JavaScript-based plots that can be deployed on the web or integrated into web frameworks like Flask or Django.

5. **pandas.plotting**:

- The **pandas.plotting** module provides convenient functions for creating plots directly from pandas DataFrame objects.
- It simplifies the process of visualizing data stored in DataFrame objects by automatically handling data alignment and axis labeling.
- **pandas.plotting** supports various plot types, including line plots, scatter plots, bar plots, histograms, box plots, and area plots.

6. **ggplot** (third-party library):

- **ggplot** is a Python port of the popular R package ggplot2, providing a grammar of graphics-based approach to creating visualizations.
- It offers a concise and expressive syntax for specifying plot aesthetics and layers, making it easy to create complex visualizations with minimal code.

7. **wordcloud** (third-party library):

- The **wordcloud** library allows creating word clouds, which are visual representations of word frequency in text data.
- It provides functions for generating word clouds with customizable shapes, colors, fonts, and sizes, making it easy to create visually appealing word cloud visualizations.

8. **networkx** (third-party library):

- **networkx** is a library for creating and analyzing network graphs and networks in Python.
- It offers functions for generating, visualizing, and analyzing complex networks, including social networks, biological networks, and transportation networks.

These modules, along with many others, provide powerful tools for creating a wide range of visualizations in Python. By leveraging these modules effectively, developers can create visually compelling and informative plots and charts to explore, analyze, and present data in a meaningful way. Whether for exploratory data analysis, reporting, or storytelling, data visualization plays a crucial role in extracting insights and communicating findings from data.

Managing Dependencies and Installing Packages:

One of the strengths of Python as a programming language is its rich ecosystem of third-party libraries and packages, which greatly extends its capabilities beyond what is available in the Python Standard Library. Managing dependencies and installing packages is a fundamental aspect of Python development, and there are several tools and techniques available for this purpose. Let's explore them in detail:

1. **pip**:
    - **pip** is the standard package manager for Python, and it comes pre-installed with most Python distributions.
    - It allows developers to easily install, upgrade, and uninstall Python packages from the Python Package Index (PyPI), as well as from other package repositories.
    - Common **pip** commands include:
        - **pip install <package_name>**: Installs a package from PyPI.
        - **pip install -r requirements.txt**: Installs packages listed in a requirements file.
        - **pip install --upgrade <package_name>**: Upgrades an installed package to the latest version.
        - **pip uninstall <package_name>**: Uninstalls a package.
2. **virtualenv**:
    - **virtualenv** is a tool for creating isolated Python environments, allowing developers to install and manage dependencies separately for each project.

- It helps avoid conflicts between dependencies from different projects and ensures reproducible environments.
- Common **virtualenv** commands include:
  - **virtualenv <env_name>**: Creates a new virtual environment.
  - **source <env_name>/bin/activate** (on Unix): Activates the virtual environment.
  - **deactivate**: Deactivates the current virtual environment.

3. **venv** (Python 3.3+):

- **venv** is a built-in module in Python 3 for creating virtual environments, similar to **virtualenv**.
- It provides similar functionalities to **virtualenv** but is included as part of the Python Standard Library, making it more accessible and convenient.
- Common **venv** commands include:
  - **python -m venv <env_name>**: Creates a new virtual environment.
  - **source <env_name>/bin/activate** (on Unix): Activates the virtual environment.
  - **deactivate**: Deactivates the current virtual environment.

4. **pipenv**:

- **pipenv** is a higher-level tool that combines the functionalities of **pip** and **virtualenv**, providing a more streamlined and user-friendly experience for managing dependencies.
- It automatically creates and manages virtual environments for each project, as well as generates and updates a **Pipfile** and **Pipfile.lock** to track dependencies.
- Common **pipenv** commands include:
  - **pipenv install <package_name>**: Installs a package and updates **Pipfile** and **Pipfile.lock**.

- **pipenv install --dev <package_name>**: Installs a package as a development dependency.
- **pipenv shell**: Activates the virtual environment.

5. **Conda**:
   - Conda is another popular package and environment manager for Python and other programming languages like R.
   - It allows for creating isolated environments and installing packages from the Conda repository, as well as from other sources like PyPI and Anaconda Cloud.
   - Conda is often used in data science and scientific computing projects due to its extensive support for scientific libraries and packages.

6. **Dependency Files**:
   - Projects typically include a file to specify their dependencies, often named **requirements.txt**, **Pipfile**, or **environment.yml**.
   - These files list all the required packages and their versions, allowing for easy installation and replication of the project's environment on different machines.
   - Developers can generate and update these files using tools like **pip freeze**, **pipenv lock**, or **conda env export**.

In summary, managing dependencies and installing packages is a crucial aspect of Python development, and there are multiple tools and techniques available to streamline this process. Whether using **pip**, **virtualenv**, **venv**, **pipenv**, Conda, or other tools, developers have options to suit their preferences and project requirements. By properly managing dependencies, developers can ensure consistent and reproducible environments for their projects, facilitating collaboration, deployment, and maintenance.

Installing Packages Using Pip:

pip is the default package manager for Python, designed to simplify the process of installing, upgrading, and managing dependencies for

Python projects. It interacts with the Python Package Index (PyPI), a repository of Python packages contributed by the Python community. Here's a comprehensive guide on managing dependencies and installing packages using pip:

Installing Packages:

- Installing packages with pip is straightforward. You can install a package by running the following command in your terminal or command prompt:

pip install <package_name>

For example, to install the popular requests library for making HTTP requests, you would run:

pip install requests

Specifying Package Versions:

- You can specify a particular version of a package to install by appending the version number after the package name. For example:

pip install requests==2.25.1

You can also specify a version range using comparison operators. For example, to install requests version 2.25.x, you would run:

pip install requests>=2.25.0,<2.26.0

Installing Packages from Requirement Files:

- You can maintain a list of project dependencies in a text file, commonly named **requirements.txt**. Each line in the file represents a package requirement in the format **<package_name>==<version>**.
- To install all dependencies listed in a requirements file, you can run:

pip install -r requirements.txt
Upgrading Packages:

- To upgrade an already installed package to the latest version, you can use the **--upgrade** flag. For example:

pip install --upgrade <package_name>
Uninstalling Packages:

- To uninstall a package, you can use the **uninstall** command followed by the package name. For example:

pip uninstall <package_name>
Listing Installed Packages:

- You can list all installed packages along with their versions using the **list** command:

pip list
Searching for Packages:

- You can search for packages available on PyPI using the **search** command followed by a search term. For example:

pip search <search_term>
Freezing Installed Packages:

- You can generate a **requirements.txt** file containing a list of currently installed packages and their versions using the **freeze** command:

pip freeze > requirements.txt

Using Constraints Files:

- Constraints files allow you to specify upper bounds on package versions, ensuring compatibility with known-good versions of dependencies. You can use the **--constraint** option to install packages according to a constraints file.

Proxy Configuration:

- If you're behind a proxy, you may need to configure pip to use the proxy server. This can be done by setting environment variables like **http_proxy** and **https_proxy**, or by configuring pip directly using the **--proxy** option.

By leveraging pip effectively, developers can manage project dependencies efficiently and ensure that their Python projects have access to the required packages. Whether it's installing, upgrading, or uninstalling packages, pip provides a robust and user-friendly interface for managing Python packages.

Installing Packages Using Virtual Environments:

Virtual environments are isolated environments that allow you to install and manage dependencies separately for each project, preventing conflicts between different project requirements. Python provides built-in support for creating virtual environments through the **venv** module. Here's a comprehensive guide on managing dependencies and installing packages using virtual environments:

Creating a Virtual Environment:

- You can create a virtual environment for your project using the **venv** module. Navigate to your project directory in the terminal or command prompt and run:

```
python -m venv <env_name>
```

Replace **<env_name>** with the name you want to give to your virtual environment. For example:

python -m venv myenv

Activating the Virtual Environment:

- Once the virtual environment is created, you need to activate it to start using it. The activation process varies depending on your operating system:
    - On Unix/Linux/Mac:

source <env_name>/bin/activate

On Windows:

<env_name>\Scripts\activate

After activation, you'll see the name of the virtual environment displayed in the terminal or command prompt, indicating that you are now working within the virtual environment.

Installing Packages:

- With the virtual environment activated, you can use pip to install packages as usual. For example:

pip install <package_name>

Installed packages will be isolated within the virtual environment and won't affect the global Python environment or other virtual environments.

Listing Installed Packages:

- To see a list of installed packages within the virtual environment, you can use the **pip list** command. This will show all packages installed in the current virtual environment along with their versions.

Specifying Dependencies:

- You can specify the dependencies for your project in a **require-ments.txt** file, just like you would in a non-virtual environment setup. It's recommended to create and maintain this file to document the dependencies of your project.
- After activating the virtual environment, you can install the dependencies listed in the **requirements.txt** file using:

pip install -r requirements.txt
Deactivating the Virtual Environment:

- When you're done working on your project, you can deactivate the virtual environment by running:

Deactivate
This will return you to the global Python environment, and you'll no longer see the virtual environment name in the terminal or command prompt.
Sharing the Environment:

- You can share the virtual environment with other developers by providing them with the **requirements.txt** file. They can recreate the exact environment by creating a new virtual environment and installing the dependencies listed in the file.

Deleting the Virtual Environment:

- If you no longer need the virtual environment, you can simply delete it by deleting the corresponding directory. Be cautious when doing this, as it will permanently remove the virtual environment and all installed packages.

By using virtual environments, developers can maintain clean and isolated environments for their Python projects, ensuring that dependencies are managed efficiently and project requirements are met without interference from other projects or the global Python environment.

14

Chapter 7: Advanced Topics in Python

Python is a versatile programming language that offers a wide range of features and capabilities beyond the basics. Advanced topics in Python encompass a variety of concepts and techniques that enable developers to write more efficient, robust, and scalable code. Let's explore some of these advanced topics in detail:

1. **Decorators:**
   - Decorators are a powerful feature in Python that allows you to modify or extend the behavior of functions or methods without changing their code.
   - They are implemented using functions that take another function as input, modify it, and return a new function.
   - Decorators are commonly used for adding logging, caching, authentication, or error handling to functions, among other tasks.

2. **Generators and Iterators:**

- Generators and iterators provide a way to work with sequences of data in a memory-efficient and lazy-evaluated manner.
- Generators are functions that yield values one at a time, allowing for the creation of custom iterable objects.
- Iterators are objects that implement the iterator protocol, allowing them to be iterated over using a for loop or consumed using functions like **next()**.

3. **Concurrency and Parallelism**:
   - Python offers several libraries and modules for concurrent and parallel programming, allowing you to execute multiple tasks simultaneously to improve performance.
   - Threading and multiprocessing are two common approaches to concurrency and parallelism in Python.
   - Libraries like **threading**, **concurrent.futures**, **asyncio**, and **multiprocessing** provide high-level interfaces for working with threads, processes, and asynchronous tasks.

4. **Metaprogramming**:
   - Metaprogramming refers to writing code that manipulates other parts of the program, such as classes, functions, or modules, at runtime.
   - Techniques like decorators, class decorators, context managers, and metaclasses enable metaprogramming in Python.
   - Metaprogramming can be used to automate repetitive tasks, implement domain-specific languages (DSLs), or create frameworks and libraries with dynamic behavior.

5. **Functional Programming**:
   - Functional programming is a programming paradigm that emphasizes the use of pure functions, immutability, and higher-order functions.

- Python supports functional programming features like lambda functions, map, filter, and reduce functions, as well as list comprehensions and generator expressions.
- Functional programming techniques can lead to more concise, readable, and maintainable code, especially for certain types of problems.

6. **Concurrency Control and Synchronization**:
- When working with concurrent or parallel programs, it's essential to ensure proper synchronization and coordination between threads or processes to avoid race conditions and data corruption.
- Python provides synchronization primitives like locks, semaphores, conditions, and barriers for managing concurrent access to shared resources.
- Techniques like thread-safe data structures, atomic operations, and message passing can also be used to implement concurrency control in Python.

7. **Performance Optimization**:
- Python offers various tools and techniques for optimizing the performance of your code, including profiling, caching, memoization, and algorithmic improvements.
- Profiling tools like cProfile and line_profiler can help identify bottlenecks and hotspots in your code.
- Techniques like memoization (caching the results of expensive function calls) and algorithmic optimizations (reducing time and space complexity) can significantly improve the performance of your Python programs.

8. **Debugging and Testing**:
- Effective debugging and testing are essential for ensuring the correctness and reliability of your Python code.
- Python provides built-in debugging tools like pdb (Python Debugger) and traceback for diagnosing and fixing errors.

- Testing frameworks like unittest, pytest, and doctest enable automated testing of Python code, including unit tests, integration tests, and functional tests.

9. **Asynchronous Programming**:
   - Asynchronous programming allows you to write non-blocking, concurrent code that can handle multiple tasks simultaneously without blocking the execution of other tasks.
   - Python's asyncio module provides a high-level asynchronous programming framework based on coroutines, allowing you to write asynchronous code using the async/await syntax.
   - Asynchronous programming is particularly useful for I/O-bound and network-intensive applications, where waiting for external resources can lead to wasted CPU cycles.

10. **Advanced Data Structures and Algorithms**:
    - Python offers a rich collection of built-in data structures like sets, dictionaries, and collections modules, as well as third-party libraries like NumPy, Pandas, and SciPy for working with arrays, matrices, and dataframes.
    - Advanced algorithms and data structures like trees, graphs, heaps, and dynamic programming can be implemented in Python using built-in data types or third-party libraries like networkx and sortedcontainers.

By mastering these advanced topics in Python, developers can write more efficient, maintainable, and scalable code, tackle complex problems, and build high-performance applications across a wide range of domains. Whether you're working on web development, data analysis, scientific computing, or systems programming, a deep understanding of these advanced concepts will elevate your Python skills to the next level.

Concurrency And Parallelism in Python:

Concurrency and parallelism are essential concepts in modern computing, allowing developers to execute multiple tasks simultaneously to improve performance and responsiveness. Python provides several approaches and libraries for implementing concurrency and parallelism, each suited for different use cases and scenarios. Let's delve into these advanced topics in detail:

1. **Threading**:
   - Threading is a concurrency model where multiple threads of execution run within the same process, sharing the same memory space.
   - Python's **threading** module provides a high-level interface for creating and managing threads.
   - Threads are lightweight, and context switching between them is relatively inexpensive, making them suitable for I/O-bound tasks and operations that involve waiting for external resources like network requests or disk I/O.

2. **Multiprocessing**:
   - Multiprocessing is a parallelism model where multiple processes run concurrently, each with its own memory space.
   - Python's **multiprocessing** module allows you to create and manage processes, which run in separate memory spaces and can execute code in parallel.
   - Multiprocessing is suitable for CPU-bound tasks and operations that can benefit from parallel execution, such as intensive mathematical computations or data processing tasks.

3. **Asynchronous Programming**:
   - Asynchronous programming is a concurrency model where tasks are executed independently, allowing the program

to continue executing other tasks while waiting for asynchronous operations to complete.

- Python's **asyncio** module provides an event loop-based framework for asynchronous programming, built on top of coroutines and the async/await syntax.
- Asynchronous programming is particularly well-suited for I/O-bound tasks and applications that rely heavily on non-blocking I/O operations, such as web servers, network clients, or asynchronous APIs.

4. **Concurrency Control and Synchronization**:
   - When working with concurrent or parallel programs, it's essential to ensure proper synchronization and coordination between threads or processes to avoid race conditions, deadlocks, and data corruption.
   - Python provides synchronization primitives like locks, semaphores, conditions, and barriers for managing concurrent access to shared resources.
   - Techniques like thread-safe data structures, atomic operations, and message passing can also be used to implement concurrency control in Python.

5. **Concurrency Patterns and Best Practices**:
   - When designing concurrent or parallel programs, it's essential to follow best practices and use appropriate concurrency patterns to ensure correctness, performance, and maintainability.
   - Common concurrency patterns include thread pooling, producer-consumer pattern, worker pool pattern, and pipeline pattern.
   - Using these patterns helps avoid common pitfalls and design flaws in concurrent and parallel programs, leading to more robust and scalable solutions.

6. **Performance Considerations**:

- When choosing between threading, multiprocessing, or asynchronous programming, it's essential to consider the performance characteristics and trade-offs of each approach.
- Threading is lightweight and suitable for I/O-bound tasks but may suffer from the Global Interpreter Lock (GIL) limitation in CPython.
- Multiprocessing provides true parallelism but incurs higher overhead due to process creation and inter-process communication.
- Asynchronous programming offers excellent scalability for I/O-bound tasks but may introduce complexity and require careful handling of shared resources.

7. **Debugging and Testing**:
  - Debugging concurrent and parallel programs can be challenging due to their non-deterministic nature and potential for race conditions and synchronization issues.
  - Python provides debugging tools like pdb (Python Debugger) and traceback for diagnosing and fixing errors in concurrent and parallel code.
  - Testing frameworks like unittest, pytest, and doctest enable automated testing of concurrent and parallel code, including unit tests, integration tests, and stress tests.

By mastering concurrency and parallelism in Python, developers can write more efficient, scalable, and responsive applications that leverage the full potential of modern computing hardware. Whether building web servers, data processing pipelines, or real-time applications, a deep understanding of these advanced concepts is essential for tackling complex concurrency challenges effectively.

Threading:

Threading is a concurrency model in Python that allows multiple threads of execution to run within the same process, sharing the same memory space. Threads are lightweight, and context switching between them is relatively inexpensive, making them suitable for tasks that are I/O-bound or involve waiting for external resources like network requests or disk I/O. Here's a comprehensive guide to threading in Python:

The threading Module:

- Python's standard library provides the **threading** module for working with threads. It offers a high-level interface for creating and managing threads within your Python programs.
- To use threading, you need to import the **threading** module:

import threading

Creating Threads:

- You can create threads by subclassing the **threading.Thread** class and implementing the **run()** method. Alternatively, you can pass a target function to the **Thread** constructor.
- Here's how you can create a thread using both approaches:

```
# Subclassing threading.Thread
class MyThread(threading.Thread):
def run(self):
print("Thread running")
# Using target function
def my_function():
print("Thread running")
thread = threading.Thread(target=my_function)
```

Starting and Joining Threads:

- After creating a thread object, you can start it by calling the **start()** method. This will invoke the **run()** method or the target function in a separate thread of execution.

- You can wait for a thread to complete its execution by calling the **join()** method. This blocks the calling thread until the target thread finishes execution.
- Here's an example of starting and joining a thread:

```
thread.start()
thread.join()
```

Thread Synchronization:

- When multiple threads access shared resources concurrently, it's essential to ensure proper synchronization to avoid race conditions and data corruption.
- Python provides synchronization primitives like locks, semaphores, conditions, and barriers for managing concurrent access to shared resources.
- You can use the **Lock** class from the **threading** module to create locks and enforce mutual exclusion:

```
lock = threading.Lock()
# Acquiring the lock
lock.acquire()
try:
# Access shared resource
finally:
# Releasing the lock
lock.release()
```

Thread Safety and Global Interpreter Lock (GIL):

- Python's Global Interpreter Lock (GIL) is a mutex that protects access to Python objects, preventing multiple threads from executing Python bytecodes simultaneously.
- While the GIL limits true parallelism in multi-threaded Python programs, it doesn't prevent threads from running concurrently

and can still provide benefits for I/O-bound tasks and certain CPU-bound tasks.

- To achieve parallelism in CPU-bound tasks, you can use the **multiprocessing** module, which creates separate processes with their own GIL

Debugging and Testing:

- Debugging multi-threaded Python programs can be challenging due to their non-deterministic nature and potential for race conditions and synchronization issues.
- Python provides debugging tools like pdb (Python Debugger) and traceback for diagnosing and fixing errors in multi-threaded code.
- Testing frameworks like unittest, pytest, and doctest enable automated testing of multi-threaded code, including unit tests, integration tests, and stress tests.

Threading in Python provides a convenient way to introduce concurrency into your applications, enabling them to perform multiple tasks concurrently and take advantage of multi-core processors. By understanding the threading module and best practices for thread synchronization, you can write efficient and scalable Python programs that leverage the power of concurrent execution.

Multiprocessing:

Multiprocessing is a parallelism model in Python that allows multiple processes to run concurrently, each with its own memory space. Unlike threading, multiprocessing enables true parallelism by leveraging multiple CPU cores, making it suitable for CPU-bound tasks and operations that can benefit from parallel execution. Here's a comprehensive guide to multiprocessing in Python:

The multiprocessing Module:

- Python's standard library provides the **multiprocessing** module for working with processes. It offers a high-level interface for creating and managing processes within your Python programs.
- To use multiprocessing, you need to import the **multiprocessing** module:

```
import multiprocessing
```

Creating Processes:

- You can create processes by instantiating the **Process** class and passing a target function to the constructor. The target function will be invoked in a separate process.
- Here's how you can create a process:

```
def my_function():
print("Process running")
process = multiprocessing.Process(target=my_function)
```

Starting and Joining Processes:

- After creating a process object, you can start it by calling the **start()** method. This will invoke the target function in a separate process.
- You can wait for a process to complete its execution by calling the **join()** method. This blocks the calling process until the target process finishes execution.
- Here's an example of starting and joining a process:

```
process.start()
process.join()
```

Interprocess Communication (IPC):

- Processes in Python do not share memory by default, so inter-process communication (IPC) mechanisms are required for communication between processes.
- Python's **multiprocessing** module provides several IPC mechanisms, including pipes, queues, shared memory, and synchronization primitives like locks, semaphores, conditions, and barriers.
- Queues are commonly used for passing data between processes in a producer-consumer pattern:

```
queue = multiprocessing.Queue()
# Producer process
queue.put(data)
# Consumer process
data = queue.get()
```

Pool of Processes:

- Creating and managing individual processes can be cumbersome, especially when dealing with a large number of tasks. Multiprocessing provides a convenient **Pool** class for managing a pool of worker processes.
- The **Pool** class allows you to parallelize the execution of a function across multiple processes, distributing the workload evenly among the available CPU cores.
- Here's an example of using a pool of processes to perform parallel computation:

```
with multiprocessing.Pool() as pool:
results = pool.map(my_function, data)
```

Process Pool Executor:

- Python's **concurrent.futures** module provides a high-level interface for working with pools of threads and processes using the **ThreadPoolExecutor** and **ProcessPoolExecutor** classes.
- The **ProcessPoolExecutor** class is similar to the **Pool** class from the **multiprocessing** module but offers a more intuitive and flexible API for asynchronous execution and result handling.

Debugging and Testing:

- Debugging and testing multiprocessing Python programs can be challenging due to their concurrent and parallel nature.
- Python provides debugging tools like pdb (Python Debugger) and traceback for diagnosing and fixing errors in multiprocessing code.
- Testing frameworks like unittest, pytest, and doctest enable automated testing of multiprocessing code, including unit tests, integration tests, and stress tests.

Multiprocessing in Python provides a powerful mechanism for achieving true parallelism and leveraging multiple CPU cores to improve the performance of CPU-bound tasks. By understanding the multiprocessing module and best practices for interprocess communication and synchronization, you can write efficient and scalable Python programs that take full advantage of modern multi-core processors.

Asynchronous Programming:

Asynchronous programming is a concurrency model in Python that allows you to write non-blocking, asynchronous code, enabling your program to perform multiple tasks concurrently without waiting for each task to complete before moving on to the next. This approach is particularly useful for I/O-bound tasks and applications that rely heavily on non-blocking I/O operations, such as web servers, network clients, or asynchronous APIs. Here's a comprehensive guide to asynchronous programming in Python:

The asyncio Module:

- Python's standard library provides the **asyncio** module for asynchronous programming. It offers an event loop-based framework for writing asynchronous code using coroutines and the async/await syntax.
- To use asyncio, you need to import the **asyncio** module:

```
import asyncio
```

Coroutines:

- Coroutines are special functions that can pause and resume their execution at specific points using the **await** keyword. They allow you to write asynchronous code in a synchronous style, making it easier to understand and maintain.
- Coroutines are defined using the **async def** syntax:

```
async def my_coroutine():
await asyncio.sleep(1)
print("Coroutine executed")
```

Event Loop:

- The event loop is the central component of asyncio that manages the execution of coroutines and I/O operations. It continuously monitors the state of coroutines and schedules them for execution when they are ready.
- You can create and run an event loop using the **asyncio.run()** function:

```
asyncio.run(my_coroutine())
```

Awaitable Objects:

- Awaitable objects are objects that can be awaited in an asynchronous function using the **await** keyword. They include coroutines, tasks, futures, and asynchronous iterators.
- Common awaitable objects in asyncio include **asyncio.sleep()**, **asyncio.gather()**, **asyncio.wait()**, and **asyncio.run_in_executor()**.

Async I/O Operations:

- Asynchronous I/O operations in asyncio are non-blocking and allow your program to perform I/O-bound tasks efficiently without blocking the event loop.
- Examples of asynchronous I/O operations include network requests, file I/O, database queries, and inter-process communication (IPC).

Concurrency Control:

- Asynchronous programming in Python requires proper concurrency control to avoid race conditions and ensure thread safety.
- Python's **asyncio** module provides synchronization primitives like locks, semaphores, conditions, and barriers for managing concurrent access to shared resources in asynchronous code.

Asynchronous Context Managers:

- Asynchronous context managers allow you to manage resources asynchronously using the **async with** statement. They are useful for acquiring and releasing resources in an asynchronous context, such as file handles or database connections.
- Python's **asyncio** module provides built-in asynchronous context managers like **asyncio.open()** for opening files asynchronously.

Debugging and Testing:

- Debugging asynchronous Python programs can be challenging due to their non-deterministic nature and potential for race conditions and synchronization issues.
- Python provides debugging tools like pdb (Python Debugger) and traceback for diagnosing and fixing errors in asynchronous code.
- Testing frameworks like unittest, pytest, and doctest enable automated testing of asynchronous code, including unit tests, integration tests, and functional tests.

Asynchronous programming in Python allows you to write highly scalable and responsive applications by leveraging non-blocking I/O operations and efficient event-driven concurrency. By understanding the asyncio module and best practices for writing asynchronous code, you can build high-performance Python applications that handle thousands of concurrent connections with ease.

Exploring Python's Networking Capabilities:

Python provides powerful networking capabilities through its standard library and third-party modules, enabling developers to create a wide range of networked applications, including web servers, clients, chat servers, network utilities, and more. Here's a comprehensive guide to exploring Python's networking capabilities:

Socket Programming:

- Socket programming is the foundation of networking in Python, allowing communication between processes over a network. Python's **socket** module provides a low-level interface for creating and interacting with sockets.

- Sockets can be used for both TCP (Transmission Control Protocol) and UDP (User Datagram Protocol) communication.
- TCP sockets provide reliable, connection-oriented communication, while UDP sockets offer fast, connectionless communication.

Creating TCP Servers and Clients:

- Python's **socket** module allows you to create TCP servers and clients for establishing network connections and exchanging data.
- A TCP server listens for incoming connections from clients and handles them using sockets, while a TCP client initiates a connection to a server and communicates with it.
- Here's an example of creating a simple TCP server and client in Python:

```python
# TCP server
import socket
server_socket = socket.socket(socket.AF_INET, socket.SOCK_STREAM)
server_socket.bind(('localhost', 8888))
server_socket.listen(5)
client_socket, addr = server_socket.accept()
data = client_socket.recv(1024)
print('Received:', data.decode())
# TCP client
import socket
client_socket = socket.socket(socket.AF_INET, socket.SOCK_STREAM)
client_socket.connect(('localhost', 8888))
client_socket.sendall(b'Hello, server')
```

Creating UDP Servers and Clients:

- Similarly, you can create UDP servers and clients using Python's **socket** module. UDP is a connectionless protocol that provides fast, unreliable communication.
- UDP servers and clients work by sending and receiving datagrams (packets) over the network.
- Here's an example of creating a simple UDP server and client in Python:

```
# UDP server
import socket
server_socket = socket.socket(socket.AF_INET, socket.SOCK_DGRAM)
server_socket.bind(('localhost', 8888))
data, addr = server_socket.recvfrom(1024)
print('Received:', data.decode())
# UDP client
import socket
client_socket = socket.socket(socket.AF_INET, socket.SOCK_DGRAM)
client_socket.sendto(b'Hello, server', ('localhost', 8888))
```

HTTP and HTTPS Client:

- Python's **http.client** module provides an HTTP client interface for making HTTP requests to web servers.
- Additionally, the **requests** library is a popular third-party module that simplifies HTTP requests and responses, making it easier to work with web APIs and services.

Creating Web Servers:

- Python's **http.server** module allows you to create simple HTTP servers for serving web pages, handling HTTP requests, and processing form submissions.

- Frameworks like Flask, Django, and FastAPI provide more advanced features and functionality for building web applications and APIs.

Web Scraping:

- Python provides several libraries like BeautifulSoup, Scrapy, and requests-html for web scraping, allowing you to extract data from web pages and automate web interactions.
- Web scraping is useful for various tasks, including data collection, content extraction, price monitoring, and web testing.

Networking Libraries:

- In addition to the standard library, Python has a rich ecosystem of third-party networking libraries and frameworks for building networked applications.
- Popular networking libraries include Twisted, asyncio, Tornado, gevent, and socket.io.

Security Considerations:

- When working with networking in Python, it's essential to consider security implications and follow best practices to prevent vulnerabilities like injection attacks, cross-site scripting (XSS), and cross-site request forgery (CSRF).
- Python's **ssl** module provides support for SSL/TLS encryption, allowing you to secure network communications over HTTPS and other secure protocols.

By exploring Python's networking capabilities, developers can build robust and scalable networked applications for various use cases, from simple client-server interactions to complex web services and distributed systems. Whether you're building a real-time chat application, a web scraper, or a network monitoring tool, Python provides the tools and libraries necessary to tackle networking challenges effectively.

Sockets:

Sockets are the building blocks of network communication in Python, enabling processes to communicate over a network using TCP (Transmission Control Protocol) or UDP (User Datagram Protocol). Python's **socket** module provides a powerful and flexible API for creating and interacting with sockets. Here's a comprehensive guide to exploring sockets in Python:

Socket Basics:

- Sockets are endpoints for communication between two machines over a network. They allow processes to send and receive data across a network connection.
- Python's **socket** module provides a low-level interface for creating and interacting with sockets.
- Sockets can be used for both TCP and UDP communication, depending on the desired characteristics of the connection (reliability vs. speed).

Creating Sockets:

- You can create a socket in Python by calling the **socket()** function from the **socket** module and specifying the address family and socket type.
- The address family typically corresponds to the protocol family, such as **AF_INET** for IPv4 or **AF_INET6** for IPv6. The socket type can be **SOCK_STREAM** for TCP or **SOCK_DGRAM** for UDP.
- Here's an example of creating a TCP socket:

```
import socket
```

```
# Create a TCP socket
server_socket = socket.socket(socket.AF_INET, socket.SOCK_STREAM)
```

Binding and Listening:

- For servers, you need to bind the socket to a specific address and port using the **bind()** method. This allows the server to listen for incoming connections on that address.
- After binding, the server socket can start listening for incoming connections using the **listen()** method, specifying the maximum number of queued connections.
- Here's how you can bind and listen for incoming connections on a server socket:

```
# Bind the socket to a specific address and port
server_socket.bind(('localhost', 8888))
# Listen for incoming connections
server_socket.listen(5)
```

Accepting Connections:

- Once the server socket is listening, it can accept incoming connections from clients using the **accept()** method. This method blocks until a client connects to the server.
- The **accept()** method returns a new socket object representing the connection to the client, along with the client's address and port.
- Here's how you can accept incoming connections on a server socket:

```
# Accept incoming connections
client_socket, client_address = server_socket.accept()
```

Connecting to Servers:

- For clients, you need to connect the socket to the server's address and port using the **connect()** method. This establishes a connection to the server and allows the client to send and receive data.
- Here's how you can connect a client socket to a server:

```
# Connect the socket to the server
client_socket.connect(('localhost', 8888))
```

Sending and Receiving Data:

- Once a connection is established, both the client and server sockets can send and receive data using the **send()** and **recv()** methods.
- The **send()** method sends data over the socket, while the **recv()** method receives data from the socket. Both methods can handle binary data (bytes).
- Here's how you can send and receive data over a socket:

```
# Send data
client_socket.send(b'Hello, server')
# Receive data
data = client_socket.recv(1024)
```

Closing Sockets:

- It's important to properly close sockets after use to release system resources and ensure clean shutdown of connections.
- You can close a socket by calling the **close()** method on the socket object.
- Here's how you can close a socket:

```
# Close the socket
server_socket.close()
```

Sockets provide a powerful mechanism for network communication in Python, allowing developers to build a wide range of networked applications, from simple client-server interactions to complex distributed systems. By mastering sockets and understanding the fundamentals of network programming, developers can create efficient, scalable, and reliable networked applications in Python.

HTTP Requests:

HTTP (Hypertext Transfer Protocol) is the foundation of communication on the World Wide Web. Python provides several ways to send HTTP requests and handle responses, allowing developers to interact with web servers, consume APIs, and scrape web pages. Here's a comprehensive guide to exploring HTTP requests in Python:

Using the http.client Module:

- Python's standard library includes the **http.client** module, which provides a low-level interface for making HTTP requests to web servers.
- You can create an HTTP connection, send requests, and handle responses using the classes and methods provided by **http.client**.
- Here's an example of making an HTTP GET request using **http.client**:

```python
import http.client
# Create an HTTP connection
connection = http.client.HTTPConnection("example.com")
# Send an HTTP GET request
connection.request("GET", "/")
# Get the response
response = connection.getresponse()
print(response.status, response.reason)
# Read the response body
data = response.read()
print(data.decode())
```

Using the urllib.request Module:

- Python's **urllib.request** module provides a higher-level interface for making HTTP requests and handling responses.
- It simplifies the process of making HTTP requests by encapsulating the details of creating connections, sending requests, and processing responses.
- Here's how you can make an HTTP GET request using **urllib.request**:

```
import urllib.request
# Make an HTTP GET request
response = urllib.request.urlopen("http://example.com")
# Read the response body
data = response.read()
print(data.decode())
```

Using the requests Library:

- The **requests** library is a popular third-party library for making HTTP requests in Python. It provides a more user-friendly and feature-rich interface compared to the standard library modules.
- With **requests**, you can easily make GET, POST, PUT, DELETE, and other types of HTTP requests, set headers, handle cookies, and more.
- Here's an example of making an HTTP GET request using **requests**:

```
import requests
# Make an HTTP GET request
response = requests.get("http://example.com")
# Check the status code
print(response.status_code)
# Read the response body
print(response.text)
```

Handling HTTP Responses:

- When making HTTP requests, it's essential to handle the responses properly. This includes checking the status code, reading the response body, and processing any headers or cookies.
- Most HTTP client libraries in Python provide methods and properties for accessing the response status code, headers, cookies, and body.

Authentication and Authorization:

- Python's HTTP client libraries support various authentication methods, including basic authentication, digest authentication, OAuth, and API keys.
- You can include authentication credentials in HTTP requests using headers or query parameters, depending on the authentication method required by the server.

SSL/TLS Encryption:

- Python's HTTP client libraries support SSL/TLS encryption for secure communication over HTTPS.
- SSL/TLS encryption ensures that HTTP requests and responses are encrypted to protect sensitive information from eavesdropping and tampering.

By exploring Python's networking capabilities for making HTTP requests, developers can interact with web servers, consume web APIs, and scrape web pages efficiently and effectively. Whether using the standard library modules like **http.client** and **urllib.request** or third-party libraries like **requests**, Python provides powerful tools for working with HTTP in a variety of applications.

Web APIs:

Web APIs (Application Programming Interfaces) are interfaces that allow different software applications to communicate with each other over the internet. They enable developers to access and manipulate data from remote servers, perform various operations, and integrate services into their applications. Python provides powerful tools and libraries for interacting with web APIs, making it easy to consume data and services from a wide range of sources. Here's a comprehensive guide to exploring web APIs in Python:

Understanding Web APIs:

- Web APIs are endpoints exposed by web servers that allow clients to interact with the server and perform specific operations, such as retrieving data, updating resources, or executing actions.
- Web APIs use standard protocols like HTTP and communicate using formats like JSON (JavaScript Object Notation) or XML (eXtensible Markup Language) for data interchange.
- There are different types of web APIs, including RESTful APIs, SOAP APIs, GraphQL APIs, and more. RESTful APIs, which follow the principles of Representational State Transfer (REST), are the most common and widely used type of web APIs.

Making API Requests:

- Python provides various libraries and tools for making HTTP requests to web APIs, such as **http.client**, **urllib.request**, and the **requests** library.
- To make a request to a web API, you typically need to specify the HTTP method (e.g., GET, POST, PUT, DELETE), the API endpoint URL, any required headers or parameters, and optionally, request body data.
- Here's an example of making a GET request to a web API using the **requests** library:

```python
import requests
# Make a GET request to a web API
```

```
response = requests.get('https://api.example.com/data')
# Check the status code
if response.status_code == 200:
# Process the response data (e.g., JSON)
data = response.json()
print(data)
else:
print('Error:', response.status_code)
```

Handling Authentication:

- Many web APIs require authentication to access protected resources or perform certain actions. Python's HTTP client libraries support various authentication methods, including basic authentication, OAuth, API keys, and token-based authentication.
- You can include authentication credentials in API requests using headers, query parameters, or request body data, depending on the authentication method required by the API.

Parsing API Responses:

- Once you receive a response from a web API, you need to parse and extract the relevant data from the response body.
- Most web APIs return data in JSON or XML format, which can be easily parsed and converted into native Python data structures (e.g., dictionaries, lists) using built-in modules like **json** or third-party libraries like **xml.etree.ElementTree**.

Error Handling:

- When interacting with web APIs, it's important to handle errors and exceptions gracefully. This includes handling network errors, server errors (e.g., HTTP status codes indicating errors), and client errors (e.g., invalid requests).

- Python's HTTP client libraries provide mechanisms for catching and handling errors and exceptions, such as timeouts, connection errors, and specific HTTP status codes.

Rate Limiting and Throttling:

- Some web APIs enforce rate limiting or throttling to prevent abuse and ensure fair usage of their resources. Rate limiting restricts the number of requests a client can make within a specified time period.
- Python applications interacting with web APIs should adhere to any rate limits or throttling rules specified by the API provider to avoid being blocked or banned.

Exploring API Documentation:

- API documentation provides detailed information about the available endpoints, request methods, parameters, authentication requirements, response formats, and usage examples.
- Before using a web API, developers should carefully read and understand its documentation to ensure proper usage and integration with their applications.

By exploring Python's networking capabilities for interacting with web APIs, developers can access a vast array of data and services available on the web and build powerful, data-driven applications. Whether consuming data from social media platforms, weather services, financial APIs, or IoT devices, Python provides the tools and libraries necessary to access and manipulate web API resources efficiently and effectively.

Introduction To GUI Programming Using Libraries:

Graphical User Interface (GUI) programming involves creating interactive applications with graphical elements such as windows, buttons, menus, and dialog boxes. GUI applications provide a user-friendly interface for users to interact with software, making it easier to perform tasks and visualize data. Python offers several libraries and frameworks for GUI programming, each with its own features and capabilities. Here's an introduction to GUI programming in Python using some of the most popular libraries:

Tkinter:

- Tkinter is Python's standard library for GUI programming, providing a simple and easy-to-use interface for creating desktop applications.
- Tkinter is based on the Tk GUI toolkit, which originated as the standard GUI toolkit for the Tcl programming language.
- With Tkinter, you can create windows, add widgets (such as buttons, labels, and entry fields), handle events, and organize the layout of your application.
- Here's a simple example of creating a Tkinter window with a button:

```python
import tkinter as tk
# Create a Tkinter window
root = tk.Tk()
# Create a button widget
button = tk.Button(root, text="Click Me")
# Pack the button widget into the window
button.pack()
# Start the Tkinter event loop
root.mainloop()
```

PyQt and **PySide:**

- PyQt and PySide are Python bindings for the Qt framework, a powerful and feature-rich GUI toolkit written in C++.
- Qt provides a comprehensive set of tools for building cross-platform applications with native-looking user interfaces.
- PyQt and PySide allow you to create desktop applications with advanced features such as custom widgets, multimedia support, 2D and 3D graphics, and internationalization.
- Here's an example of creating a PyQt window with a button:

```python
from PyQt5.QtWidgets import QApplication, QPushButton
# Create a QApplication instance
app = QApplication([])
# Create a QPushButton instance
button = QPushButton("Click Me")
# Show the button
button.show()
# Run the application event loop
app.exec_()
```

wxPython:

- wxPython is a Python binding for the wxWidgets toolkit, a mature and cross-platform GUI framework written in C++.
- wxPython allows you to create native-looking GUI applications for Windows, macOS, and Linux.
- It provides a wide range of widgets, including buttons, text controls, list boxes, tree controls, and more.
- Here's an example of creating a wxPython window with a button:

```python
import wx
# Create a wx.App instance
app = wx.App()
# Create a wx.Frame instance
frame = wx.Frame(None, title="Hello, wxPython")
# Create a wx.Button instance
```

```
button = wx.Button(frame, label="Click Me")
# Show the frame
frame.Show()
# Run the application event loop
app.MainLoop()
```

Kivy:

- Kivy is an open-source Python library for developing multi-touch applications, including mobile apps, using a natural user interface (NUI).
- It provides a cross-platform framework for building applications that run on desktop, mobile, and embedded devices.
- Kivy uses a declarative syntax for creating user interfaces and supports gestures, animations, and multitouch input.
- Here's an example of creating a Kivy application with a button:

```
from kivy.app import App
from kivy.uix.button import Button
class MyApp(App):
def build(self):
return Button(text='Hello, Kivy')
if __name__ == '__main__':
MyApp().run()
```

GUI programming in Python opens up a world of possibilities for creating interactive and visually appealing applications. Whether you're building desktop utilities, data visualization tools, or mobile apps, Python's GUI libraries provide the tools and flexibility you need to bring your ideas to life. Experiment with different libraries and frameworks to find the one that best suits your needs and preferences.

Implementing unit testing

Unit testing is a critical aspect of software development that involves testing individual units or components of code to ensure they work correctly in isolation. Python provides robust tools and frameworks for writing and running unit tests, allowing developers to automate the testing process and catch bugs early in the development cycle. Here's a comprehensive guide to implementing unit testing in Python projects:

Introduction to Unit Testing:

- Unit testing is a software testing technique where individual units or components of code are tested in isolation to verify that they perform as expected.
- Units can be functions, methods, classes, or modules. The goal of unit testing is to validate the behavior of each unit in isolation from the rest of the system.

The unittest Module:

- Python's standard library includes the **unittest** module, which provides a framework for writing and running unit tests.
- **unittest** supports test automation, test discovery, test fixtures, and various assertion methods for validating expected outcomes.
- Tests are organized into test cases, which are subclasses of the **unittest.TestCase** class.

Writing Test Cases:

- Test cases are written as methods within a test case class. Each test method should start with the word **test** to be recognized as a test case by the test runner.
- Inside each test method, you use assertion methods such as **assertEqual**, **assertTrue**, **assertFalse**, **assertRaises**, etc., to check whether the actual result matches the expected result.
- Here's an example of a simple test case using **unittest**:

```
import unittest
```

```python
def add(a, b):
return a + b
class TestAddFunction(unittest.TestCase):
def test_add_positive_numbers(self):
self.assertEqual(add(3, 4), 7)
def test_add_negative_numbers(self):
self.assertEqual(add(-3, -4), -7)
if __name__ == '__main__':
unittest.main()
```

Running Tests:

- Tests can be run using the **unittest** test runner, which can be invoked from the command line or integrated into development environments and continuous integration (CI) pipelines.
- To run tests from the command line, you can use the **-m unittest** option followed by the module name:

```
python -m unittest test_module.py
```

Test Fixtures:

- Test fixtures are setup and teardown routines that prepare the environment for running tests and clean up afterward.
- **unittest** provides methods like **setUp()** and **tearDown()** in test case classes for setting up and tearing down resources used by multiple tests.

Mocking and Patching:

- In unit testing, mocking and patching are techniques used to replace real objects or functions with mock objects or functions for testing purposes.
- Python provides libraries like **unittest.mock** and **unittest.patch** for mocking and patching objects and functions in unit tests.

Coverage Analysis:

- Code coverage analysis measures the percentage of code covered by unit tests, helping identify areas of code that are not adequately tested.
- Tools like **coverage.py** can be used to generate code coverage reports for Python projects.

By implementing unit testing in Python projects, developers can improve code quality, reduce the number of bugs, and increase confidence in the reliability and stability of their software. Unit tests serve as documentation for the behavior of individual units of code and help ensure that changes to the codebase do not introduce regressions. Investing in unit testing pays off in the long run by reducing the time and effort spent on debugging and maintenance.

Test-Driven Development (TDD):

Test-Driven Development (TDD) is a software development approach that emphasizes writing tests before writing the actual code. The process involves writing a failing test case, writing the minimum amount of code to make the test pass, and then refactoring the code to improve its design while ensuring that all tests continue to pass. TDD encourages iterative development, improves code quality, and helps produce more maintainable and reliable software. Here's a comprehensive guide to implementing TDD in Python projects:

Understanding Test-Driven Development (TDD):

- TDD is a development methodology where tests are written before the implementation code.
- The TDD cycle typically consists of three phases: Red, Green, and Refactor.
- In the Red phase, a failing test case is written to specify the desired behavior of the code.

- In the Green phase, the minimum amount of code is written to make the test case pass.
- In the Refactor phase, the code is refactored to improve its design while ensuring that all tests continue to pass.

Advantages of TDD:

- TDD promotes better code design by encouraging developers to focus on the interface and behavior of their code before implementation.
- It helps catch bugs early in the development process, leading to fewer defects and higher code quality.
- TDD improves test coverage and documentation by ensuring that tests are written for every piece of functionality.
- It encourages small, incremental changes, which makes it easier to manage and maintain codebases over time.

Setting Up the Testing Environment:

- Before starting with TDD, it's essential to set up a testing environment for your Python project.
- Python's **unittest** module or third-party libraries like **pytest** can be used for writing and running tests.
- Install the testing framework of your choice using **pip**:

pip install pytest

Writing the First Test:

- Begin by writing a failing test case that specifies the desired behavior of the code.
- Use descriptive test names that communicate the expected behavior of the code.

- Write assertions that validate the expected outcomes of the code under test.

Refactoring:

- Once the test case passes, refactor the code to improve its design without changing its behavior.
- Look for opportunities to simplify the code, remove duplication, and improve readability.
- Refactoring should be done incrementally, with each refactoring step followed by running the tests to ensure that no regressions occur.

Writing Additional Tests:

- After making the initial test case pass, write additional test cases to cover edge cases, error conditions, and other scenarios.
- Use TDD to drive the development of new features and functionality, writing failing tests for each new requirement before implementing the corresponding code.

Maintaining the Test Suite:

- Regularly run the test suite to ensure that all tests continue to pass as the codebase evolves.
- Update and refactor tests as necessary to keep them in sync with changes to the code.
- Aim for a balance between test coverage and test maintainability, focusing on testing critical and complex areas of the codebase.

Integrating TDD into the Development Workflow:

- Make TDD an integral part of the development process by practicing it consistently throughout the project.
- Encourage collaboration and code review among team members to ensure that tests are well-written and effective.
- Use continuous integration (CI) tools to automate the execution of tests and provide feedback on code changes.

By implementing Test-Driven Development (TDD) in Python projects, developers can improve code quality, reduce bugs, and build more reliable and maintainable software. TDD encourages a disciplined and incremental approach to development, leading to better-designed code and increased confidence in the correctness of the software.

15

Chapter 8: Real-World Applications and Projects

Python's versatility, ease of use, and extensive ecosystem of libraries make it a popular choice for developing a wide range of real-world applications and projects across various domains. From web development and data science to machine learning, automation, and beyond, Python's capabilities empower developers to tackle diverse challenges and create innovative solutions. Here's a comprehensive overview of real-world applications and projects in Python:

Web Development:

- Python frameworks like Django and Flask are widely used for building web applications, APIs, and content management systems (CMS).
- Django provides a full-featured and batteries-included framework for building complex, scalable web applications with built-in authentication, ORM (Object-Relational Mapping), and templating.
- Flask is a lightweight and flexible micro-framework that allows developers to build simple to complex web applications with

minimal boilerplate code.

Data Science and Machine Learning:

- Python's rich ecosystem of libraries, including NumPy, Pandas, Matplotlib, and Scikit-learn, makes it a popular choice for data science and machine learning projects.
- Data scientists and researchers use Python to analyze and visualize data, build predictive models, and deploy machine learning solutions in various domains such as finance, healthcare, e-commerce, and more.
- TensorFlow and PyTorch are widely used deep learning frameworks in Python for building and training neural networks for tasks like image recognition, natural language processing (NLP), and reinforcement learning.

Automation and Scripting:

- Python's simplicity and readability make it well-suited for writing automation scripts and performing repetitive tasks.
- Python scripts can automate system administration tasks, data processing, file manipulation, web scraping, and more.
- Tools like Selenium and BeautifulSoup enable web scraping and automation of browser interactions, while libraries like OpenCV facilitate computer vision tasks.

Desktop GUI Applications:

- Python offers several libraries and frameworks for developing desktop graphical user interface (GUI) applications.
- Libraries like Tkinter, PyQt, and wxPython provide tools for creating cross-platform desktop applications with native-looking interfaces.
- Python's versatility allows developers to build desktop applications for various purposes, including text editors, image viewers, games, scientific visualization tools, and more.

Game Development:

- Python is increasingly used in game development for prototyping, scripting, and building game engines.

- Pygame is a popular library for building 2D games in Python, providing tools for handling graphics, sound, input devices, and more.
- Unity3D and Godot Engine support scripting in Python, allowing developers to create 2D and 3D games with Python as the scripting language.

Internet of Things (IoT):

- Python is gaining popularity in the IoT space for its ease of use and extensive libraries for interfacing with hardware and sensors.
- Libraries like Raspberry Pi GPIO, Adafruit CircuitPython, and MicroPython enable developers to build IoT projects using single-board computers and microcontrollers.
- Python's networking capabilities make it well-suited for developing IoT applications for home automation, smart agriculture, industrial monitoring, and more.

Scientific Computing and Simulation:

- Python is widely used in scientific computing, simulation, and numerical analysis due to its extensive libraries and tools.
- Libraries like SciPy, SymPy, and NumPy provide functions and algorithms for scientific computing, linear algebra, optimization, symbolic mathematics, and more.
- Python is used in academic research, engineering, physics, chemistry, and other scientific disciplines for modeling complex systems, simulating experiments, and analyzing data.

Natural Language Processing (NLP):

- Python's natural language processing (NLP) libraries, including NLTK (Natural Language Toolkit), spaCy, and Gensim, enable developers to analyze and process human language data.
- NLP techniques are used in applications such as text classification, sentiment analysis, machine translation, chatbots, information retrieval, and summarization.

Cybersecurity and Penetration Testing:

- Python is used in cybersecurity for developing tools and scripts for network scanning, vulnerability assessment, penetration testing, and malware analysis.
- Libraries like Scapy and Metasploit provide frameworks for network packet manipulation and exploitation testing, while tools like Nmap and Burp Suite offer Python APIs for automation.

Cloud Computing and DevOps:

- Python is widely used in cloud computing and DevOps for automating infrastructure management, deployment, and monitoring tasks.
- Tools like Ansible, Terraform, and Kubernetes leverage Python for automation and orchestration of cloud resources, containers, and microservices.

These are just a few examples of the diverse applications and projects that Python is used for in the real world. Python's simplicity, versatility, and vibrant community continue to drive innovation across industries, making it a valuable skill for developers and organizations alike. Whether you're building web applications, analyzing data, controlling hardware, or exploring cutting-edge technologies, Python provides the tools and frameworks to bring your ideas to life.

Building Practical Applications and Projects:

One of the most effective ways to solidify your Python skills is by building practical applications and projects. Not only does this approach reinforce your understanding of Python concepts and syntax, but it also provides valuable hands-on experience in solving real-world problems. Here's a comprehensive guide to building practical applications and projects to enhance your Python proficiency:

1. **Identify a Project Idea:**
   - Start by identifying a project idea that interests you and aligns with your learning goals.

- Choose a project that challenges you but is also achievable based on your current skill level.
- Consider projects in areas such as web development, data analysis, automation, game development, IoT, cybersecurity, or any other domain that piques your interest.

2. **Plan and Design**:
   - Once you have a project idea, create a plan and design for your application.
   - Define the project requirements, features, and functionality.
   - Break down the project into smaller tasks or modules to make it more manageable.
   - Design the user interface (if applicable) and outline the data structures and algorithms needed to implement the project.

3. **Set Up Your Development Environment**:
   - Set up your development environment with the necessary tools and libraries for your project.
   - Install Python and any third-party libraries or frameworks required for your project.
   - Choose an Integrated Development Environment (IDE) or code editor that you're comfortable with, such as PyCharm, Visual Studio Code, or Jupyter Notebook.

4. **Start Coding**:
   - Begin coding your project incrementally, starting with the core functionality and gradually adding more features.
   - Write clean, modular, and well-documented code that follows Python coding conventions and best practices.
   - Use version control systems like Git to track changes and collaborate with others (if applicable).
   - Test your code frequently as you develop, using unit tests or manual testing to ensure that each component works as expected.

5. **Iterate and Refine**:
   - Iterate on your project by continuously testing, debugging, and refining your code.
   - Solicit feedback from peers, mentors, or online communities to identify areas for improvement.
   - Refactor your code to improve readability, performance, and maintainability.
   - Keep the project scope manageable and avoid feature creep by focusing on essential functionality first.

6. **Document Your Work**:
   - Document your project by writing clear and comprehensive documentation.
   - Include instructions for installing and using your application, explanations of key features, and any relevant information for other developers or users.
   - Document the code itself with comments, docstrings, and inline explanations to make it easier for others (and yourself) to understand.

7. **Deploy and Share**:
   - Once your project is complete and tested, consider deploying it to a live environment (if applicable).
   - Share your project with others by publishing it on platforms like GitHub, GitLab, or Bitbucket.
   - Contribute your project to open-source communities or share it with potential employers as part of your portfolio.

8. **Reflect and Learn**:
   - Reflect on your project experience and identify lessons learned, challenges faced, and areas for improvement.
   - Use feedback from users or collaborators to iterate on your project and incorporate new features or enhancements.
   - Continue learning and exploring new technologies, frameworks, and tools to further expand your Python skills.

By building practical applications and projects, you not only reinforce your Python skills but also gain valuable experience in software development, problem-solving, and project management. Whether you're a beginner looking to gain hands-on experience or an experienced developer seeking to expand your portfolio, building projects is an effective way to grow as a Python programmer and demonstrate your abilities to others.

Developing Web Applications Using Frameworks:Top of Form

Web development is one of the most common and practical uses of Python, and frameworks like Django and Flask simplify the process of building web applications by providing a structured and efficient way to handle common tasks. Whether you're building a simple blog, a complex e-commerce platform, or a scalable web service, Django and Flask empower developers to create robust and feature-rich web applications. Here's a comprehensive guide to developing web applications using Django or Flask:

1. **Choose a Framework**:
    - Django and Flask are two popular web frameworks in Python, each with its own strengths and use cases.
    - Django is a high-level web framework that follows the "batteries-included" philosophy, providing a full-featured toolkit for building complex web applications quickly.
    - Flask is a lightweight and flexible micro-framework that offers more freedom and flexibility, allowing developers to choose the components they need and build applications with minimal boilerplate code.
    - Choose the framework that best suits your project requirements, development style, and familiarity with the framework.
2. **Project Setup**:

- Once you've chosen a framework, set up your project environment by installing the framework and any additional dependencies.
- Use virtual environments to isolate your project dependencies and prevent conflicts with system-wide packages:

  pip install Django

  or

  pip install flask

3. **Define Your Application Structure**:
   - Define the structure of your web application by organizing your code into models, views, and templates (in Django) or routes, templates, and static files (in Flask).
   - In Django, models represent the data structure of your application, views handle the request-response cycle, and templates define the presentation layer.
   - In Flask, routes map URLs to view functions, templates render HTML pages, and static files (e.g., CSS, JavaScript) serve static content.

4. **Database Integration**:
   - Integrate a database into your web application to store and retrieve data.
   - Django provides built-in support for ORM (Object-Relational Mapping) with its own ORM layer, allowing you to define database models using Python classes and interact with the database using high-level APIs.
   - Flask supports various database libraries and ORMs, including SQLAlchemy, Peewee, and Flask-SQLAlchemy, giving you the flexibility to choose the database solution that best fits your needs.

5. **Routing and URL Configuration**:
   - Define URL patterns and routing rules to map incoming requests to the appropriate view functions or handlers.

- In Django, URL routing is configured using the **urls.py** module, where you define URL patterns and associate them with corresponding views.
- In Flask, URL routing is defined using the **@app.route** decorator to specify URL patterns and map them to view functions.

6. **Template Rendering**:
   - Use templates to generate dynamic HTML content and render it to the client's web browser.
   - Django's template engine allows you to define templates using Django's template language, which includes template tags, filters, and inheritance for building reusable and modular templates.
   - Flask uses Jinja2 as its default template engine, which provides similar functionality to Django's template engine, including template inheritance, loops, conditionals, and macros.

7. **Handling Forms and User Input**:
   - Implement forms to collect and validate user input in your web application.
   - Both Django and Flask provide mechanisms for handling forms, including form classes, form validation, and CSRF protection.
   - Django's form handling is built-in and includes form classes, model forms, and form validation using built-in validators.
   - Flask offers form handling through extensions like Flask-WTF, which provides forms, CSRF protection, and validation features similar to Django's forms.

8. **Authentication and Authorization**:
   - Implement user authentication and authorization to secure your web application and restrict access to certain resources.

- Django provides a built-in authentication system with features like user registration, login, logout, password reset, and permissions.
- Flask offers authentication and authorization through extensions like Flask-Login and Flask-Security, which provide similar functionality to Django's authentication system.

9. **Static and Media Files**:

- Serve static files (e.g., CSS, JavaScript, images) and media files (e.g., user-uploaded images, files) to the client's web browser.
- Configure static and media file handling in your web application settings to serve static files from the **STATIC_ROOT** directory (in Django) or static folder (in Flask) and media files from the **MEDIA_ROOT** directory (in Django) or media folder (in Flask).

10. **Testing and Debugging**:

- Write unit tests to verify the functionality of your web application and catch bugs early in the development process.
- Use Django's built-in testing framework or Flask's testing utilities to write and run tests for your application.
- Debug your web application using debugging tools provided by Django or Flask, including error pages, logging, and debugging middleware.

11. **Deployment**:

- Deploy your web application to a production environment once it's ready for deployment.
- Choose a web server (e.g., Apache, Nginx) and deployment platform (e.g., Heroku, AWS, DigitalOcean) based on your project requirements and budget.
- Configure your web server and deployment environment to serve your web application securely and efficiently.

12. **Continuous Integration and Deployment (CI/CD)**:

- Set up continuous integration and deployment pipelines to automate the process of building, testing, and deploying your web application.
- Use CI/CD services like GitHub Actions, Travis CI, or GitLab CI to automate the deployment process and ensure that changes are deployed to production safely and efficiently.

Building web applications using frameworks like Django or Flask is an excellent way to hone your Python skills and gain hands-on experience in web development. By following best practices, leveraging the features of these frameworks, and continuously learning and improving, you can create robust and scalable web applications that meet the needs of your users and clients.

The following are coding examples to develop web applications using either Django or Flask.

Web development is a crucial aspect of software engineering, and Python offers powerful frameworks like Django and Flask to streamline the process. These frameworks provide robust tools for building web applications, from handling routing and authentication to interacting with databases and rendering dynamic content. Let's delve into developing web applications using Django and Flask with comprehensive coding examples:

1. **Setting Up the Development Environment:**
   Before diving into coding, ensure you have Python installed on your system. You can install Django or Flask using pip:
   # Install Django
   pip install django
   # Install Flask
   pip install flask

2. **Creating a Django Project:**
   To create a new Django project, run the following command in your terminal:

```
django-admin startproject myproject
```

This command will create a directory named **myproject** with the following structure:

```
myproject/
manage.py
myproject/
__init__.py
settings.py
urls.py
asgi.py
wsgi.py
```

3. **Defining Routes and Views (Django):**

In Django, routes are defined in the **urls.py** file, and views are defined in the **views.py** file within each Django app. Let's define a simple route and view:

```python
# myapp/views.py
from django.http import HttpResponse
def index(request):
    return HttpResponse("Hello, Django!")
# myproject/urls.py
from django.urls import path
from myapp import views
urlpatterns = [
path(", views.index, name='index'),
]
```

4. **Creating a Flask App:**

To create a Flask app, you can define routes directly within your Python script. Here's a simple example:

```python
# app.py
from flask import Flask
app = Flask(__name__)
@app.route('/')
def index():
```

```
return 'Hello, Flask!'
if __name__ == '__main__':
app.run(debug=True)
```

5. **Handling Form Submissions (Flask):**

Flask provides extensions like Flask-WTF for handling forms. Let's create a simple contact form using Flask-WTF:

```
# forms.py
from flask_wtf import FlaskForm
from wtforms import StringField, SubmitField
from wtforms.validators import DataRequired
class ContactForm(FlaskForm):
name = StringField('Name', validators=[DataRequired()])
email = StringField('Email', validators=[DataRequired()])
message = StringField('Message', validators=[DataRequired()])
submit = SubmitField('Submit')
# app.py
from flask import Flask, render_template, redirect, url_for
from forms import ContactForm
app = Flask(__name__)
app.config['SECRET_KEY'] = 'your_secret_key'
@app.route('/', methods=['GET', 'POST'])
def contact():
form = ContactForm()
if form.validate_on_submit():
# Process form submission (save to database, send email, etc.)
return redirect(url_for('success'))
return render_template('contact.html', form=form)
@app.route('/success')
def success():
return 'Form submitted successfully!'
if __name__ == '__main__':
app.run(debug=True)
```

6. **Templating (Jinja2 for Flask, Django Templates for Django):**

Both Flask and Django support templating engines for rendering dynamic content. Here's an example using Jinja2 for Flask:

```
<!-- templates/contact.html -->
<!DOCTYPE html>
<html>
<head>
<title>Contact Form</title>
</head>
<body>
<h1>Contact Us</h1>
<form method="POST">
{{ form.hidden_tag() }}
{{ form.name.label }} {{ form.name() }}
{{ form.email.label }} {{ form.email() }}
{{ form.message.label }} {{ form.message() }}
{{ form.submit() }}
</form>
</body>
</html>
```

7. **Database Integration (Django ORM and Flask-SQLAlchemy):**

Django comes with its built-in ORM for interacting with databases, while Flask can use SQLAlchemy for database operations. Let's define a simple model and query it in Django:

```
# myapp/models.py
from django.db import models
class Book(models.Model):
title = models.CharField(max_length=100)
author = models.CharField(max_length=50)
publication_date = models.DateField()
# Querying the database
```

```python
books = Book.objects.all()
```

In Flask, you can define models using SQLAlchemy:

```python
# models.py
from flask_sqlalchemy import SQLAlchemy
db = SQLAlchemy()
class Book(db.Model):
id = db.Column(db.Integer, primary_key=True)
title = db.Column(db.String(100))
author = db.Column(db.String(50))
publication_date = db.Column(db.Date)
# Querying the database
books = Book.query.all()
```

8. **Authentication and Authorization (Django Authentication vs. Flask-Login):**

Django provides a built-in authentication system, while Flask offers extensions like Flask-Login for handling user authentication. Here's a quick example using Flask-Login:

```python
# app.py
from flask import Flask, render_template, redirect, url_for
from flask_login import LoginManager, login_user, UserMixin
app = Flask(__name__)
app.secret_key = 'your_secret_key'
login_manager = LoginManager(app)
class User(UserMixin):
def __init__(self, id):
self.id = id
@login_manager.user_loader
def load_user(user_id):
return User(user_id)
@app.route('/login')
def login():
user = User(1)
login_user(user)
return redirect(url_for('index'))
```

```
@app.route('/')
def index():
return 'You are logged in!'
if __name__ == '__main__':
app.run(debug=True)
```

9. **Deployment:**

Once your application is ready, you can deploy it to a web server or cloud platform. For Django, you can deploy using platforms like Heroku, PythonAnywhere, or AWS Elastic Beanstalk. For Flask, the process is similar, and you can also use platforms like Gunicorn or uWSGI along with Nginx or Apache.

By following these examples and exploring the documentation of Django and Flask, you can build robust and scalable web applications tailored to your specific requirements. Whether you're developing a small project or a large-scale application, Django and Flask provide the tools and flexibility needed to succeed in web development with Python.

Creating Data Science and Machine Learning:

<u>Using NumPy:</u>

Data science and machine learning have become integral parts of various industries, ranging from finance and healthcare to marketing and entertainment. Python, with libraries like NumPy, Pandas, and Scikit-learn, has emerged as the leading choice for developing data-driven applications and machine learning models. Here's a comprehensive guide to creating data science and machine learning projects using NumPy, along with coding examples:

1. **Setting Up Your Environment**:
    ○ Install Python and the necessary libraries, including NumPy, Pandas, Matplotlib, and Scikit-learn, using pip:

pip install numpy pandas matplotlib scikit-learn

- Optionally, you can use Anaconda or Miniconda to create a virtual environment with all the required packages.

1. **Loading and Exploring Data**:
    - Start by loading your dataset into a NumPy array or a Pandas DataFrame.
    - Use NumPy's **loadtxt()** or **genfromtxt()** functions to load data from text files, or Pandas' **read_csv()** function to load data from CSV files.
    - Explore the data using descriptive statistics, visualization, and data profiling techniques to gain insights into its structure, distribution, and relationships.
    - Here's an example of loading and exploring data using NumPy and Matplotlib:

```python
import numpy as np
import matplotlib.pyplot as plt
# Load data
data = np.loadtxt('data.csv', delimiter=',')
# Basic statistics
print('Mean:', np.mean(data))
print('Standard Deviation:', np.std(data))
# Visualization
plt.hist(data, bins=20)
plt.xlabel('Value')
plt.ylabel('Frequency')
plt.title('Histogram of Data')
plt.show()
```

2. **Data Preprocessing**:
    - Preprocess the data to handle missing values, outliers, and categorical variables.

- Use techniques like imputation, normalization, and one-hot encoding to prepare the data for modeling.
- Pandas provides convenient functions for data preprocessing, such as **fillna()**, **dropna()**, **replace()**, and **get_dummies()**.

3. **Building Machine Learning Models**:
   - Choose an appropriate machine learning algorithm based on the problem you're trying to solve and the nature of your data.
   - Split the data into training and testing sets using techniques like cross-validation or holdout validation.
   - Train the model on the training data using Scikit-learn's **fit()** function, and evaluate its performance on the testing data using metrics like accuracy, precision, recall, and F1-score.
   - Here's an example of building and evaluating a classification model using Scikit-learn:

```python
from sklearn.model_selection import train_test_split
from sklearn.linear_model import LogisticRegression
from sklearn.metrics import accuracy_score
# Split data into features (X) and target variable (y)
X = data[:, :-1]
y = data[:, -1]
# Split data into training and testing sets
X_train, X_test, y_train, y_test = train_test_split(X, y, test_size=0.2, random_state=42)
# Initialize and train the model
model = LogisticRegression()
model.fit(X_train, y_train)
# Make predictions
y_pred = model.predict(X_test)
# Evaluate model performance
```

```
accuracy = accuracy_score(y_test, y_pred)
print('Accuracy:', accuracy)
```

4. **Hyperparameter Tuning**:
   - Fine-tune your machine learning models by adjusting their hyperparameters using techniques like grid search or random search.
   - Scikit-learn provides tools like **GridSearchCV** and **RandomizedSearchCV** for hyperparameter tuning.
   - Experiment with different hyperparameter values to optimize the model's performance.

5. **Model Deployment**:
   - Once you've trained and validated your model, deploy it to production to make predictions on new data.
   - You can deploy your model as a web service using frameworks like Flask or Django, or as a REST API using tools like Flask-RESTful or FastAPI.
   - Serialize your trained model using libraries like Pickle or Joblib, and load it into your deployment environment to make predictions in real-time.

6. **Monitoring and Maintenance**:
   - Monitor your deployed model's performance over time and retrain it periodically with new data to ensure its accuracy and reliability.
   - Implement logging, error handling, and version control mechanisms to track changes and troubleshoot issues effectively.
   - Continuously evaluate your model's performance against business metrics and adjust its parameters or features as needed.

7. **Example Project: Predicting Housing Prices**:
   - As an example, let's consider a project where we aim to predict housing prices based on features like square footage, number of bedrooms, and location.

- ○ We'll use a dataset containing housing information and build a regression model to predict the prices.
- ○ Here's a simplified code snippet for loading the data and training a linear regression model using Scikit-learn:

```
import numpy as np
import pandas as pd
from sklearn.model_selection import train_test_split
from sklearn.linear_model import LinearRegression
from sklearn.metrics import mean_squared_error
# Load data
data = pd.read_csv('housing.csv')
# Split data into features (X) and target variable (y)
X = data.drop('price', axis=1)
y = data['price']
# Split data into training and testing sets
X_train, X_test, y_train, y_test = train_test_split(X, y, test_size=0.2, random_state=42)
# Initialize and train the model
model = LinearRegression()
model.fit(X_train, y_train)
# Make predictions
y_pred = model.predict(X_test)
# Evaluate model performance
rmse = np.sqrt(mean_squared_error(y_test, y_pred))
print('Root Mean Squared Error:', rmse)
```

8. **Conclusion**:

- ○ Data science and machine learning projects using libraries like NumPy offer exciting opportunities to solve real-world problems and make data-driven decisions.
- ○ By following best practices in data preprocessing, model building, and deployment, you can create robust and reliable solutions that drive business value and innovation.

9. **Further Exploration**:

- Experiment with different algorithms, feature engineering techniques, and evaluation metrics to improve your model's performance.
- Explore advanced topics like deep learning, ensemble methods, and reinforcement learning to tackle more complex problems and domains.
- Collaborate with peers, participate in competitions, and contribute to open-source projects to gain practical experience and expand your knowledge in data science and machine learning.

Using Panadas:

1. **Importing Pandas and Loading Data:**

- Begin by importing the Pandas library into your Python environment:

```
import pandas as pd
```

- Load your dataset into a Pandas DataFrame using one of the available functions, such as **pd.read_csv()**, **pd.read_excel()**, or **pd.read_sql()**.
- Here's an example of loading a CSV file into a DataFrame:

```
# Load a CSV file into a Pandas DataFrame
df = pd.read_csv('data.csv')
```

1. **Exploratory Data Analysis (EDA):**

- Perform exploratory data analysis to gain insights into your dataset and understand its structure, content, and distribution.

- Use Pandas methods and functions to examine the first few rows of the dataset, check for missing values, and calculate summary statistics.
- Here are some common EDA tasks with Pandas:

```python
# Display the first few rows of the DataFrame
print(df.head())
# Check for missing values
print(df.isnull().sum())
# Calculate summary statistics
print(df.describe())
```

1. **Data Cleaning and Preprocessing**:

- Clean and preprocess the data to handle missing values, outliers, and inconsistencies.
- Use Pandas methods like **fillna()**, **dropna()**, and **replace()** to handle missing values and outliers.
- Perform data normalization, standardization, or scaling as needed.
- Here's an example of cleaning and preprocessing data with Pandas:

```python
# Handle missing values by filling with mean
df.fillna(df.mean(), inplace=True)
# Remove outliers
df = df[(df['column'] > lower_threshold) & (df['column'] < upper_threshold)]
# Normalize data
df_normalized = (df - df.min()) / (df.max() - df.min())
```

1. **Data Visualization**:

- Visualize your data using plotting libraries like Matplotlib or Seaborn, which seamlessly integrate with Pandas.
- Create various types of plots, including histograms, scatter plots, box plots, and line plots, to explore relationships and patterns in the data.
- Here's an example of creating a histogram using Pandas and Matplotlib:

```python
# Plot a histogram of a numerical variable
df['column'].hist()
plt.xlabel('Column')
plt.ylabel('Frequency')
plt.title('Histogram of Column')
plt.show()
```

1. **Feature Engineering**:

- Perform feature engineering to create new features or transform existing ones to improve model performance.
- Use Pandas to create new columns, apply mathematical transformations, or extract information from existing features.
- Here's an example of feature engineering with Pandas:

```python
# Create a new feature based on existing columns
df['new_feature'] = df['feature1'] + df['feature2']
# Apply a mathematical transformation to a feature
df['transformed_feature'] = np.log(df['feature'] + 1)
```

1. **Model Building and Evaluation**:

- Build machine learning models using libraries like Scikit-learn, integrating Pandas for data preprocessing and feature selection.
- Split the data into training and testing sets, train the model on the training data, and evaluate its performance on the testing data.

- Use Pandas to prepare the data for modeling and evaluate model performance.
- Here's an example of model building and evaluation with Scikit-learn and Pandas:

```python
from sklearn.model_selection import train_test_split
from sklearn.linear_model import LogisticRegression
from sklearn.metrics import accuracy_score
# Split data into features and target variable
X = df.drop('target', axis=1)
y = df['target']
# Split data into training and testing sets
X_train, X_test, y_train, y_test = train_test_split(X, y, test_size=0.2, random_state=42)
# Initialize and train the model
model = LogisticRegression()
model.fit(X_train, y_train)
# Make predictions on the testing data
y_pred = model.predict(X_test)
# Evaluate model performance
accuracy = accuracy_score(y_test, y_pred)
print('Accuracy:', accuracy)
```

1. **Iterate and Improve**:

- Iterate on your model by experimenting with different algorithms, hyperparameters, and feature engineering techniques.
- Use cross-validation, grid search, or other optimization methods to fine-tune your models.
- Continuously evaluate and validate your model's performance using techniques like cross-validation and performance metrics.

8. Deployment and Productionization:

- Once you have a satisfactory model, deploy it to a production environment for real-world use.

- Create APIs or web applications using frameworks like Flask or Django to serve predictions or insights generated by your model.
- Implement monitoring and logging to track the model's performance and behavior in production.
- Update and maintain your model as new data becomes available or business requirements change.

By leveraging Pandas and other Python libraries, you can create robust data science and machine learning projects that extract actionable insights from your data and drive informed decision-making. Whether you're exploring datasets, building predictive models, or deploying machine learning solutions, Pandas provides the tools and functionality you need to succeed in your data-driven projects.

Using Scikit-Learn:

Scikit-learn is one of the most popular machine learning libraries in Python, known for its simple and efficient tools for data mining and data analysis. It provides a wide range of algorithms for classification, regression, clustering, dimensionality reduction, and more, making it ideal for building data science and machine learning projects. Here's a comprehensive guide to creating such projects with scikit-learn, along with coding examples:

1. **Importing scikit-learn and Loading Data**:
   - Begin by importing scikit-learn into your Python environment:

```
import sklearn
```

- Load your dataset into scikit-learn-compatible data structures, typically NumPy arrays or pandas DataFrames.
- Here's an example of loading a dataset from scikit-learn's built-in datasets:

```
from sklearn.datasets import load_iris
```

```
iris = load_iris()
X, y = iris.data, iris.target
```

1. **Exploratory Data Analysis (EDA)**:

- Perform exploratory data analysis to understand the characteristics and distribution of your dataset.
- Use statistical summaries, visualizations, and correlation analyses to gain insights into the data.
- Here's an example of performing EDA with scikit-learn's built-in datasets:

```
print(iris.feature_names) # Print feature names
print(iris.target_names) # Print target names
print(X.shape) # Print the shape of features
```

1. **Data Preprocessing**:

- Preprocess the data to handle missing values, scale features, and encode categorical variables if necessary.
- Use preprocessing techniques like standardization, normalization, and one-hot encoding.
- Here's an example of preprocessing data with scikit-learn's preprocessing module:

```
from sklearn.preprocessing import StandardScaler, OneHotEncoder
scaler = StandardScaler()
X_scaled = scaler.fit_transform(X)
```

1. **Model Selection and Training**:

- Select appropriate machine learning algorithms for your problem domain and dataset.

- Split the data into training and testing sets using scikit-learn's **train_test_split()** function.
- Train the selected models on the training data.
- Here's an example of splitting data and training a classifier with scikit-learn:

```
from sklearn.model_selection import train_test_split
from sklearn.tree import DecisionTreeClassifier
X_train, X_test, y_train, y_test = train_test_split(X_scaled, y, test_size=0.2, random_state=42)
model = DecisionTreeClassifier()
model.fit(X_train, y_train)
```

1. **Model Evaluation**:

- Evaluate the trained models using appropriate performance metrics such as accuracy, precision, recall, F1-score, or ROC-AUC.
- Use scikit-learn's **metrics** module to calculate these metrics.
- Here's an example of evaluating a classifier's performance with scikit-learn:

```
from sklearn.metrics import accuracy_score
y_pred = model.predict(X_test)
accuracy = accuracy_score(y_test, y_pred)
print("Accuracy:", accuracy)
```

1. **Hyperparameter Tuning and Model Selection**:

- Fine-tune model hyperparameters using techniques like grid search or randomized search.
- Select the best-performing model based on cross-validated performance scores.

- Here's an example of performing hyperparameter tuning with scikit-learn's **GridSearchCV**:

```
from sklearn.model_selection import GridSearchCV
params = {'max_depth': [3, 5, 7], 'min_samples_split': [2, 5, 10]}
grid_search = GridSearchCV(model, params, cv=5)
grid_search.fit(X_train, y_train)
best_model = grid_search.best_estimator_
```

1. **Model Deployment and Prediction**:

- Deploy the trained model to make predictions on new, unseen data.
- Save the trained model to disk using scikit-learn's **joblib** module for future use.
- Here's an example of saving and loading a trained model with **joblib**:

```
from joblib import dump, load
dump(best_model, 'best_model.joblib')
loaded_model = load('best_model.joblib')
```

1. **Iterate and Improve**:
   - Iterate on your model by experimenting with different algorithms, feature engineering techniques, and hyper-parameters.
   - Continuously evaluate and improve model performance based on feedback from stakeholders or new data.
2. **Real-World Applications**:
   - Apply your machine learning model to real-world problems such as predicting customer churn, detecting fraud, classifying diseases, or recommending products.

○ Monitor and maintain the deployed model, retraining it periodically with new data to keep it up-to-date and accurate.

By leveraging scikit-learn's powerful algorithms and tools, you can build robust data science and machine learning projects that extract valuable insights from your data and drive informed decision-making. Whether you're exploring datasets, building predictive models, or deploying machine learning solutions, scikit-learn provides the functionality and flexibility you need to succeed in your data-driven projects.

Building Automation Scripts, Web Scrapers, And Data Analysis Tools:

Automation scripts, web scrapers, and data analysis tools are essential components in various real-world applications, from simplifying repetitive tasks to gathering insights from vast amounts of data on the web. Python, with its versatility and rich ecosystem of libraries, such as BeautifulSoup for web scraping and pandas for data analysis, is well-suited for building these tools. Here's a comprehensive guide to creating automation scripts, web scrapers, and data analysis tools in Python, along with coding examples:

1. **Automation Scripts**:

   Automation scripts are programs designed to perform specific tasks automatically, reducing manual effort and increasing efficiency. These scripts can automate tasks such as file manipulation, data processing, system maintenance, and more.

   Example: Automating File Management

   ```
   import os
   import shutil
   # Source and destination directories
   source_dir = 'source_folder'
   destination_dir = 'destination_folder'
   ```

```
# Iterate over files in the source directory
for filename in os.listdir(source_dir):
if filename.endswith('.txt'):
# Copy text files from source to destination directory
shutil.copy(os.path.join(source_dir, filename), destination_dir)
```

2. **Web Scrapers**:

   Web scrapers are tools that extract data from websites, allowing users to collect information for analysis, research, or other purposes. Python libraries like BeautifulSoup and Scrapy are commonly used for web scraping tasks.

   Example: Scraping Website Data with BeautifulSoup

```
from bs4 import BeautifulSoup
import requests
# URL of the website to scrape
url = 'https://example.com'
# Send a GET request to the URL
response = requests.get(url)
# Parse the HTML content of the page
soup = BeautifulSoup(response.text, 'html.parser')
# Extract data from specific elements
headlines = soup.find_all('h2', class_='headline')
for headline in headlines:
print(headline.text)
```

3. **Data Analysis Tools**:

   Data analysis tools are applications or scripts that process, analyze, and visualize data to derive insights and make informed decisions. Python libraries like pandas, NumPy, and Matplotlib are commonly used for data analysis tasks.

   Example: Analyzing Sales Data with Pandas

```
import pandas as pd
# Load sales data from a CSV file into a DataFrame
df = pd.read_csv('sales_data.csv')
# Perform data analysis and visualization
```

```python
total_sales = df['sales'].sum()
average_sales = df['sales'].mean()
max_sales = df['sales'].max()
# Display summary statistics
print('Total Sales:', total_sales)
print('Average Sales:', average_sales)
print('Max Sales:', max_sales)
# Plot a histogram of sales data
df['sales'].plot(kind='hist')
```

4. **Integration of APIs**:

Many automation scripts, web scrapers, and data analysis tools interact with external APIs to access additional data or perform specific actions. Python's requests library makes it easy to send HTTP requests and interact with APIs.

Example: Accessing Weather Data from an API

```python
import requests
# API endpoint for weather data
url = 'https://api.openweathermap.org/data/2.5/weather'
api_key = 'your_api_key'
# Parameters for the API request
params = {'q': 'New York', 'appid': api_key}
# Send a GET request to the API endpoint
response = requests.get(url, params=params)
# Extract and display weather data from the response
data = response.json()
temperature = data['main']['temp']
print('Current Temperature in New York:', temperature)
```

5. **Error Handling and Logging**:

Robust automation scripts, web scrapers, and data analysis tools should include error handling mechanisms to handle unexpected situations gracefully. Additionally, logging functionality helps track program execution and troubleshoot issues.

Example: Error Handling and Logging

```
import logging
# Configure logging
logging.basicConfig(filename='app.log', level=logging.INFO)
try:
# Perform some operation
result = 1 / 0
except ZeroDivisionError as e:
# Log the error
logging.error(f'Error occurred: {e}')
```

6. **Testing and Documentation**:

It's crucial to test automation scripts, web scrapers, and data analysis tools thoroughly to ensure they work as expected. Additionally, providing comprehensive documentation helps users understand how to use the tools effectively.

Example: Unit Testing with pytest

```
import pytest
# Function to be tested
def add(x, y):
return x + y
# Test function
def test_add():
assert add(2, 3) == 5
assert add(0, 0) == 0
assert add(-1, 1) == 0
```

7. **Deployment and Maintenance**:

Once developed, automation scripts, web scrapers, and data analysis tools may require deployment to production environments. Additionally, regular maintenance and updates ensure that the tools remain functional and up-to-date.

By leveraging Python and its ecosystem of libraries, developers can build powerful automation scripts, web scrapers, and data analysis tools to streamline processes, extract valuable insights, and make data-driven decisions in various real-world applications.

16

Chapter 9: Best Practices and Advanced Techniques

In this chapter, we'll explore best practices and advanced techniques in Python programming. These practices are essential for writing efficient, maintainable, and scalable code. We'll cover topics such as code organization, optimization, debugging, documentation, and more. Let's delve into each aspect with detailed explanations and coding examples:

1. **Code Organization**:

- Structuring your codebase effectively improves readability, maintainability, and collaboration among developers.
- Use modules and packages to organize related functionality into separate files and directories.
- Example:

```
my_project/
├── main.py
├── utils/
│   ├── __init__.py
```

```
|   ├── helper_functions.py
├── data/
|   ├── __init__.py
|   ├── data_processing.py
└── tests/
    ├── __init__.py
    ├── test_utils.py
    └── test_data.py
```

1. **Optimization Techniques**:

- Optimizing code improves performance and reduces resource consumption.
- Use efficient data structures and algorithms for better time and space complexity.
- Example:

```python
# Using list comprehension instead of traditional loops
squares = [i ** 2 for i in range(1, 11)]
# Efficiently concatenate strings using join()
words = ['hello', 'world', 'python']
sentence = ' '.join(words)
```

1. **Debugging and Error Handling**:

- Proper debugging and error handling techniques help identify and resolve issues in code.
- Use debugging tools like Python's built-in **pdb** debugger or third-party tools like **pdbpp** for interactive debugging.
- Example:

```python
# Debugging with pdb
import pdb
```

pdb.set_trace()

- Implement robust error handling using try-except blocks and raise custom exceptions for better error messages.
- Example:

```
try:
# Risky operation
result = 10 / 0
except ZeroDivisionError as e:
# Handle the error gracefully
print("Error:", e)
```

1. **Documentation and Comments**:

- Clear and concise documentation improves code understanding and promotes reusability.
- Use docstrings to document modules, functions, classes, and methods.
- Example:

```
def add(x, y):
"""Add two numbers."""
return x + y
```

- Add inline comments to explain complex logic or to provide context for future maintainers.
- Example:

```
# Check if the number is even
if num % 2 == 0:
print("Even number")
```

1. **Version Control**:

- Version control systems like Git help manage code changes, collaborate with team members, and track project history.
- Use Git for version control and follow best practices for branching, committing, and merging code changes.
- Example:

```
# Create a new branch for feature development
git checkout -b feature-branch
# Add and commit changes
git add .
git commit -m "Implement feature XYZ"
# Merge changes into main branch
git checkout main
git merge feature-branch
```

1. **Testing**:

- Writing automated tests ensures code correctness, prevents regressions, and facilitates refactoring.
- Use testing frameworks like pytest or unittest to write and run tests.
- Example:

```
# Test function
def test_add():
assert add(2, 3) == 5
assert add(0, 0) == 0
assert add(-1, 1) == 0
```

1. **Code Reviews**:

- Conducting code reviews fosters collaboration, improves code quality, and helps identify potential issues.

- Review code changes thoroughly, provide constructive feedback, and ensure adherence to coding standards and best practices.
- Example:

```
# Code Review Checklist:
- Is the code well-documented?
- Are variable names meaningful?
- Are there any potential bugs or edge cases?
- Is the code efficient and readable?
```

By incorporating these best practices and advanced techniques into your Python development workflow, you can write high-quality, efficient, and maintainable code that meets the demands of complex projects and real-world applications.

Understanding Pythonic Code:

Pythonic code refers to code that follows the idioms and conventions of the Python programming language. Writing Pythonic code not only makes your programs more readable and maintainable but also leverages the language's features to write concise and efficient code.

1. **Use of List Comprehensions**:

   List comprehensions provide a concise and readable way to create lists in Python. They are often preferred over traditional loops for simple transformations or filtering operations.

```
# Traditional loop to create a list of squares
squares = []
for i in range(10):
squares.append(i**2)
# Equivalent list comprehension
squares = [i**2 for i in range(10)]
```

2. **Avoiding Unnecessary Loops with Generators**:

   Generators allow you to generate values lazily, avoiding the need to store all values in memory at once. This is particularly useful for large datasets or infinite sequences.

```python
# Traditional function returning a list
def square_numbers(n):
result = []
for i in range(n):
result.append(i**2)
return result
# Generator function yielding values lazily
def square_numbers(n):
for i in range(n):
yield i**2
```

3. **Utilizing Python's Built-in Functions**:

Python provides a rich set of built-in functions and modules that help you write more expressive and efficient code. Familiarizing yourself with these functions can greatly improve your productivity.

```python
# Using built-in functions like max and min
numbers = [1, 2, 3, 4, 5]
max_value = max(numbers)
min_value = min(numbers)
# Using built-in functions like sum and len
total = sum(numbers)
length = len(numbers)
```

4. **Applying Decorators for Code Reuse and Modularity**:

Decorators are a powerful feature in Python that allow you to modify or extend the behavior of functions or methods. They are commonly used for aspects such as logging, authentication, and memoization.

```python
# Decorator function to log function calls
def log_function(func):
def wrapper(*args, **kwargs):
print(f'Calling function {func.__name__} with args {args} and kwargs {kwargs}')
return func(*args, **kwargs)
```

```
return wrapper
@log_function
def add(a, b):
return a + b
```

5. **Writing Readable and Self-Documenting Code**:

Python emphasizes readability, and it's important to write code that is easy to understand for yourself and others. Use descriptive variable names, meaningful comments, and adhere to PEP 8 guidelines for code style.

```
# Clear and descriptive variable names
user_input = input('Enter your name:')
# Comments to explain the purpose of code
# Calculate the area of a rectangle
area = length * width
```

6. **Following PEP 8 Guidelines for Code Style**:

PEP 8 is the official style guide for Python code. Adhering to PEP 8 guidelines ensures consistency and readability across Python projects. You can use tools like Flake8 or pylint to check your code against PEP 8.

```
# Example of adhering to PEP 8 guidelines
def calculate_area(length, width):
return length * width
```

7. **Understanding Context Managers for Resource Management**:

Context managers, implemented using the **with** statement, provide a convenient way to manage resources such as files, database connections, or locks. They ensure that resources are properly released after their use.

```
# Using a context manager to open and close a file
with open('example.txt', 'r') as file:
contents = file.read()
```

8. **Avoiding Mutable Default Arguments**:

Mutable default arguments in function definitions can lead to unexpected behavior due to shared references. Instead, use immutable objects or **None** as default values and handle mutable objects inside the function.

```python
# Avoid mutable default arguments
def append_to_list(value, my_list=[]):
my_list.append(value)
return my_list
# Instead, use immutable default values or None
def append_to_list(value, my_list=None):
if my_list is None:
my_list = []
my_list.append(value)
return my_list
```

9. **Leveraging Python's Data Structures and Modules**:

Python provides powerful built-in data structures like dictionaries, sets, and tuples, as well as modules for common tasks such as data manipulation, networking, and concurrency. Utilize these features to write efficient and expressive code.

```python
# Using dictionary comprehensions for data manipulation
data = {'a': 1, 'b': 2, 'c': 3}
doubled_data = {key: value * 2 for key, value in data.items()}
```

By following these best practices and adopting idiomatic Python programming techniques, you can write code that is not only efficient and maintainable but also conforms to Python's philosophy of readability and simplicity. Continuously honing your skills and staying updated with the Python community will further enhance your proficiency in writing Pythonic code.

Writing Efficient and Maintainable Code:

Writing efficient and maintainable code is crucial for the success of any software project. Efficient code ensures that programs run smoothly, utilize resources effectively, and deliver optimal performance.

1. **Use Built-in Functions and Data Structures**:

   Python provides a rich set of built-in functions and data structures that are optimized for performance. Utilizing these built-ins can often lead to faster and more efficient code compared to custom implementations.

   ```python
   # Using built-in functions like sum for faster computation
   numbers = [1, 2, 3, 4, 5]
   total = sum(numbers)
   ```

2. **Choose the Right Data Structure for the Task**:

   Selecting the appropriate data structure based on the requirements of your program can significantly impact its performance. For example, use sets for membership tests and dictionaries for fast lookups.

   ```python
   # Using sets for membership tests
   unique_numbers = {1, 2, 3, 4, 5}
   if 6 not in unique_numbers:
   print("6 is not in the set")
   ```

3. **Avoid Unnecessary Computations**:

   Identify and eliminate redundant computations or unnecessary operations in your code. This includes avoiding repeated calculations and unnecessary loops.

   ```python
   # Avoiding unnecessary computations
   total = 0
   for number in range(1000000):
   total += number # Redundant addition operation
   ```

4. **Optimize Loops and Iterations**:

   Loops and iterations are common bottlenecks in code execution. Look for opportunities to optimize loops by reducing the number of iterations or using vectorized operations.

   ```python
   # Using vectorized operations for faster computation
   ```

```python
import numpy as np
numbers = np.array([1, 2, 3, 4, 5])
total = np.sum(numbers)
```

5. **Implement Algorithmic Optimization**:

   Choose efficient algorithms and data structures for solving specific problems. Understanding algorithmic complexity (time and space) helps in selecting the most suitable approach.

```python
# Using a more efficient algorithm for sorting
numbers = [5, 3, 1, 4, 2]
sorted_numbers = sorted(numbers) # Uses Timsort algorithm
```

6. **Profile and Benchmark Your Code**:

   Use profiling tools like cProfile and line_profiler to identify performance bottlenecks in your code. Benchmarking libraries like timeit can help compare the performance of different implementations.

```python
# Using cProfile to profile code
import cProfile
def my_function():
# Code to profile
pass
cProfile.run('my_function()')
```

7. **Optimize I/O Operations**:

   I/O operations, such as reading from or writing to files and databases, can often be optimized for better performance. Consider using buffered I/O, asynchronous I/O, or memory-mapped files where applicable.

```python
# Using buffered I/O for faster file operations
with open('data.txt', 'r', buffering=8192) as file:
data = file.read()
```

8. **Use Compiled Extensions for Performance-Critical Sections**:

   For performance-critical sections of code, consider using compiled extensions such as Cython or writing Python C extensions.

These can provide significant performance improvements over pure Python code.

```python
# Using Cython for performance optimization
# my_module.pyx
def my_function(int n):
cdef int total = 0
for i in range(n):
total += i
return total
```

9. **Cache Intermediate Results**:

Cache intermediate results or expensive computations to avoid recalculating them multiple times. This is particularly useful for recursive algorithms or functions with expensive computations.

```python
# Caching intermediate results to improve performance
from functools import lru_cache
@lru_cache(maxsize=None)
def fibonacci(n):
if n <= 1:
return n
return fibonacci(n - 1) + fibonacci(n - 2)
```

10. **Optimize Memory Usage**:

Be mindful of memory usage, especially when working with large datasets. Avoid unnecessary object creation, use generators instead of lists for lazy evaluation, and release resources promptly to free up memory.

```python
# Using generator expressions to conserve memory
squares = (x**2 for x in range(1000000))
```

By applying these techniques and best practices, you can write Python code that is not only efficient and performant but also maintainable and scalable. Continuously profiling and optimizing your code ensures that it meets the performance requirements of your application and provides a smooth user experience.

Exploring Advanced Debugging Techniques:

Effective debugging is a crucial skill for any Python developer. While print statements and basic breakpoints are helpful, advanced debugging techniques and tools provide deeper insights into code behavior and help identify and resolve complex issues more efficiently.

1. **Using pdb for Interactive Debugging**:

   Python's built-in debugger, **pdb** (Python Debugger), provides a powerful interactive debugging environment. It allows you to step through code, inspect variables, set breakpoints, and more.

   ```python
   import pdb
   def divide(a, b):
   pdb.set_trace() # Set a breakpoint
   return a / b
   result = divide(10, 0)
   ```

   Once the debugger is activated, you can use commands like **step**, **next**, **continue**, **print**, and **list** to navigate through the code and inspect variables.

2. **Utilizing Conditional Breakpoints**:

   Conditional breakpoints allow you to pause execution only when certain conditions are met. This is helpful for debugging specific scenarios or edge cases.

   ```python
   import pdb
   def factorial(n):
   result = 1
   for i in range(1, n + 1):
   if i == 5:
   pdb.set_trace() # Conditional breakpoint
   result *= i
   return result
   print(factorial(10))
   ```

3. **Exploring Visual Debuggers**:

   Visual debuggers, such as PyCharm's debugger or VS Code's

built-in debugger, provide a graphical interface for debugging Python code. They offer features like variable inspection, call stack visualization, and watch expressions.

4. **Using Logging for Debugging**:

Logging is a powerful tool for debugging and monitoring the execution flow of a program. By strategically placing logging statements, you can trace the flow of execution and inspect variable values.

```
import logging
logging.basicConfig(level=logging.DEBUG)
def divide(a, b):
logging.debug(f'Dividing {a} by {b}')
return a / b
result = divide(10, 0)
```

You can configure logging levels to control the verbosity of log messages.

5. **Profiling and Performance Analysis**:

Profilers like **cProfile** and **line_profiler** help identify performance bottlenecks in your code by measuring the execution time of each function and line. This is useful for optimizing code and improving efficiency.

```
import cProfile
def factorial(n):
result = 1
for i in range(1, n + 1):
result *= i
return result
cProfile.run('factorial(10000)')
```

6. **Using Remote Debugging**:

Remote debugging allows you to debug Python code running on a remote server or a different environment. Tools like **remote-pdb** or PyCharm's remote debugging feature facilitate this process.

```
# Install remote-pdb: pip install remote-pdb
import rpdb
rpdb.set_trace()
```

7. **Exploring Memory Debugging Tools**:

Memory debugging tools like **memory_profiler** or **objgraph** help identify memory leaks and excessive memory usage in Python programs. They provide insights into memory allocation and usage patterns.

```
# Install memory_profiler: pip install memory-profiler
@profile
def my_function():
# Code to profile
pass
my_function()
```

8. **Integrating Assertions for Error Checking**:

Assertions are useful for validating assumptions about code behavior during development and debugging. They help catch potential errors and inconsistencies early in the development process.

```
def divide(a, b):
assert b != 0, "Division by zero"
return a / b
result = divide(10, 0)
```

When an assertion fails, it raises an **AssertionError** with a custom error message.

9. **Using IDE Features for Debugging**:

Integrated Development Environments (IDEs) like PyCharm, VS Code, and Spyder offer a wide range of debugging features, including step-through debugging, variable inspection, and code profiling.

By mastering these advanced debugging techniques and tools, Python developers can streamline the debugging process, diagnose issues more effectively, and optimize code performance for robust and efficient software development. Continuously practicing and exploring new debugging tools will enhance your debugging skills and make you a more proficient developer.

Leveraging Design Patterns in Python Projects:

Design patterns and architectural principles play a vital role in building robust, scalable, and maintainable software systems. They provide reusable solutions to common problems and guide the overall structure and organization of code.

1. **Singleton Pattern**:

   The Singleton pattern ensures that a class has only one instance and provides a global point of access to that instance.

```python
class Singleton:
_instance = None
def __new__(cls):
if cls._instance is None:
cls._instance = super().__new__(cls)
return cls._instance
singleton_instance = Singleton()
```

2. **Factory Pattern**:

   The Factory pattern provides an interface for creating objects without specifying their concrete classes.

```python
class Shape:
def draw(self):
pass
class Circle(Shape):
def draw(self):
print("Drawing Circle")
class Rectangle(Shape):
def draw(self):
print("Drawing Rectangle")
class ShapeFactory:
```

```python
def create_shape(self, shape_type):
if shape_type == 'circle':
return Circle()
elif shape_type == 'rectangle':
return Rectangle()
factory = ShapeFactory()
circle = factory.create_shape('circle')
rectangle = factory.create_shape('rectangle')
```

3. **Observer Pattern**:

The Observer pattern defines a one-to-many dependency between objects, where changes in one object trigger updates in dependent objects.

```python
class Subject:
def __init__(self):
self._observers = []
def attach(self, observer):
self._observers.append(observer)
def notify(self, message):
for observer in self._observers:
observer.update(message)
class Observer:
def update(self, message):
print(f"Received message: {message}")
subject = Subject()
observer1 = Observer()
observer2 = Observer()
subject.attach(observer1)
subject.attach(observer2)
subject.notify("Hello Observers!")
```

4. **Model-View-Controller (MVC) Architecture**:

MVC separates the application into three interconnected components: Model (data and business logic), View (presentation layer), and Controller (handles user input and updates the model and view).

```python
class Model:
def __init__(self):
self._data = ""
def set_data(self, data):
self._data = data
def get_data(self):
return self._data
class View:
def display_data(self, data):
print(f"Displaying data: {data}")
class Controller:
def __init__(self, model, view):
self._model = model
self._view = view
def process_data(self, data):
self._model.set_data(data)
self._view.display_data(self._model.get_data())
model = Model()
view = View()
controller = Controller(model, view)
controller.process_data("Hello MVC!")
```

5. **Dependency Injection (DI):**

Dependency Injection is a technique where dependencies of a class are provided from the outside rather than created internally.

```python
class Database:
def query(self, sql):
return "Result of SQL query"
class Service:
def __init__(self, database):
self._database = database
def do_task(self):
result = self._database.query("SELECT * FROM table")
print(result)
database = Database()
```

```
service = Service(database)
service.do_task()
```

6. **RESTful API Design**:

When designing RESTful APIs, adhere to principles such as resource-based URLs, stateless communication, and standard HTTP methods (GET, POST, PUT, DELETE).

```
from flask import Flask, request, jsonify
app = Flask(__name__)
@app.route('/api/resource', methods=['GET', 'POST'])
def resource():
if request.method == 'GET':
# Retrieve resource
return jsonify({"message": "GET request"})
elif request.method == 'POST':
# Create new resource
data = request.json
return jsonify({"message": "POST request", "data": data})
if __name__ == '__main__':
app.run(debug=True)
```

7. **Domain-Driven Design (DDD)**:

DDD emphasizes a focus on the core domain and domain logic, separating it from infrastructure concerns. Use concepts like entities, value objects, aggregates, and repositories to model domain logic effectively.

```
class Order:
def __init__(self, order_id, products):
self.order_id = order_id
self.products = products
class Product:
def __init__(self, product_id, name, price):
self.product_id = product_id
self.name = name
self.price = price
class OrderRepository:
```

```python
def save_order(self, order):
# Save order to database
pass
order_repository = OrderRepository()
order = Order(order_id=1, products=[Product(1, 'Product 1', 10),
Product(2, 'Product 2', 20)])
order_repository.save_order(order)
```

By leveraging design patterns and architectural principles like the ones mentioned above, Python developers can create well-structured, maintainable, and scalable software solutions. These patterns and principles provide a solid foundation for building complex applications while promoting code reuse, separation of concerns, and flexibility. Continuously learning and applying these concepts will improve the quality and efficiency of your Python projects.

17

Chapter 10: Beyond Mastery

Congratulations on reaching a level of mastery in Python! However, learning in the field of programming is a journey that never truly ends. There's always something new to discover, explore, and master.

Books:

- "Fluent Python" by Luciano Ramalho: This book dives deep into Python's internals, teaching you how to write idiomatic, effective Python code.
- "Python Cookbook" by David Beazley and Brian K. Jones: Explore a wide range of Python recipes and best practices for common programming tasks and challenges.
- "Effective Python" by Brett Slatkin: Learn Python's best practices, patterns, and idioms for writing clean, maintainable, and efficient code.

Online Courses:

- Coursera: Offers a variety of Python courses from top universities and instructors, including "Python for Everybody" by the University of Michigan.

- Udemy: Provides numerous Python courses covering different skill levels and specializations, such as web development, data science, and machine learning.
- Pluralsight: Offers comprehensive Python learning paths and courses curated by industry experts, suitable for both beginners and advanced learners.

1. **Tutorials and Documentation**:
   - Real Python (realpython.com): A treasure trove of Python tutorials, articles, and resources covering topics ranging from basic syntax to advanced concepts like concurrency and web development.
   - Python Official Documentation: The Python documentation is an invaluable resource for understanding Python's standard library, language features, and best practices.

   Communities and Forums:
   - Stack Overflow: A vibrant community of developers where you can ask questions, share knowledge, and learn from others' experiences.
   - Reddit: Subreddits like r/learnpython, r/python, and r/programming are excellent places to seek advice, share insights, and stay updated on Python-related news and trends.
   - Python Discord Server: An active Discord community dedicated to Python programming, where you can engage in discussions, ask questions, and collaborate with fellow Python enthusiasts.

   Open-Source Contributions:
   - Contributing to open-source projects is a fantastic way to apply your Python skills, learn from experienced developers, and give back to the community. Websites like GitHub and GitLab host millions of open-source projects across various domains.

- Start by exploring beginner-friendly issues labeled "good first issue" or "help wanted" in repositories that interest you. This allows you to gain experience and contribute meaningfully to projects.

Hackathons and Coding Challenges:

- Participating in hackathons and coding challenges provides an opportunity to solve real-world problems, collaborate with peers, and sharpen your coding skills under time constraints.
- Platforms like HackerRank, LeetCode, and Codeforces host coding challenges and competitions where you can practice algorithmic problem-solving and improve your coding proficiency.

Specializations and Advanced Topics:

- Depending on your interests and career goals, consider diving deeper into specialized areas of Python, such as web development with Django or Flask, data science with libraries like Pandas and scikit-learn, or machine learning and deep learning with TensorFlow and PyTorch.
- Explore advanced topics like concurrency, parallelism, design patterns, software architecture, and cloud computing to broaden your skill set and become a well-rounded developer.

Continuing your Python journey involves a combination of self-study, hands-on practice, collaboration, and continuous learning. Embrace curiosity, stay engaged with the Python community, and keep challenging yourself with new projects and concepts. Remember, mastery is not a destination but a continuous process of growth and exploration. Happy coding!

Contributing To the Python Ecosystem:

As you progress in your Python journey and master its fundamentals and advanced concepts, you'll find numerous opportunities to contribute to the Python ecosystem and continue your learning.

Contributing to Open-Source Projects:

Contributing to open-source projects is an excellent way to give back to the Python community and gain practical experience. You can contribute by fixing bugs, adding new features, improving documentation, or helping with project management tasks.

Example: Contributing to an open-source project on GitHub

Fork the repository

Clone the forked repository to your local machine

Make changes, commit them, and push to your fork

Create a pull request to submit your changes to the original repository

Participating in Python Communities:

Joining Python communities, forums, and mailing lists allows you to connect with fellow developers, share knowledge, and seek help when needed. Communities like Python Discord, Python Forum, and Reddit's r/Python are great places to start.

Example: Participating in a Python community forum

Ask questions, answer queries, and engage in discussions

Share your projects and seek feedback

Contribute to community-driven initiatives and events

Mentoring and Teaching:

Sharing your knowledge and expertise with others by mentoring or teaching Python can be incredibly rewarding. You can mentor beginners, contribute to educational platforms, or even start your own Python tutorial series.

Example: Creating Python tutorials on YouTube or other platforms

Cover various topics, from beginner to advanced levels

Provide clear explanations, code examples, and practical exercises

Encourage interaction and feedback from viewers

Organizing and Participating in Hackathons:

Hackathons are great opportunities to collaborate with others, work on interesting projects, and contribute to the Python ecosystem. You can organize hackathons locally or participate in online hackathons organized by various communities.

Example: Participating in a Python hackathon

Form a team with other participants

Choose a project idea and start collaborating

Use Python to build a prototype or solution within the hackathon's timeframe

Showcase your project and seek feedback from judges and peers

Writing and Publishing Python Packages:

If you've developed useful libraries or tools in Python, consider packaging and publishing them on platforms like PyPI (Python Package Index). This allows other developers to benefit from your work and contributes to the Python ecosystem.

Example: Publishing a Python package on PyPI

Create a setup.py file with package metadata and dependencies

Build and package your project using setuptools

Register and upload your package to PyPI using twine

Install and use your package in other projects via pip

Contributing to Python Documentation:

Improving Python documentation ensures that it remains comprehensive, accurate, and accessible to developers worldwide. You can contribute by fixing typos, clarifying explanations, and adding examples to the official Python documentation.

Example: Contributing to Python documentation on GitHub

Fork the CPython repository

Locate the documentation file you want to modify

Make changes, commit them, and push to your fork

Create a pull request to submit your changes for review

Participating in Python Events and Conferences:

Attending Python events, conferences, and meetups provides valuable networking opportunities, allows you to stay updated on the latest trends and developments, and fosters collaboration within the community.

Example: Attending PyCon, the largest annual Python conference

Participate in keynote sessions, talks, workshops, and sprints

Network with fellow developers, speakers, and industry professionals

Share your experiences and insights with the community

Contributing to Python Enhancement Proposals (PEPs):

Python Enhancement Proposals (PEPs) are documents that propose and describe changes to the Python language and standard libraries. Contributing to PEP discussions or drafting new PEPs allows you to shape the future direction of Python.

Example: Contributing to PEP discussions on the Python-Dev mailing list

Review existing PEPs and provide feedback or suggestions

Propose new ideas or improvements to Python language features

Collaborate with other developers and core Python developers to refine PEPs

By actively contributing to the Python ecosystem, you not only enhance your skills and knowledge but also help foster a vibrant and inclusive community. Whether through code contributions, mentoring, or participation in events, each contribution plays a valuable role in advancing Python as a language and empowering developers worldwide.

Career Paths and Opportunities for Python Developers:

As you continue your journey in mastering Python, you'll find that the language opens up numerous career paths and opportunities across various industries.

Software Development:

Python developers are in high demand across the software development industry. They work on a wide range of projects, including web development, mobile app development, desktop application development, and game development. Python's versatility and ease of use make it a popular choice for building diverse software solutions.

Data Science and Machine Learning:

Python is the go-to language for data science, machine learning, and artificial intelligence projects. Python libraries like NumPy, pandas, scikit-learn, and TensorFlow provide powerful tools for data analysis, modeling, and machine learning. Python developers in this field work on tasks such as data preprocessing, predictive modeling, and building machine learning pipelines.

DevOps and Automation:

Python is widely used in DevOps and automation for tasks such as infrastructure provisioning, configuration management, continuous integration, and deployment automation. Python developers in this field write scripts and tools to automate manual tasks, streamline workflows, and improve system reliability and scalability.

Web Development:

Python frameworks like Django and Flask are popular choices for web development. Python developers in this field build dynamic websites, web applications, and APIs using frameworks that emphasize simplicity, flexibility, and scalability. They work on both backend and frontend components, integrating databases, handling user authentication, and designing responsive user interfaces.

Data Engineering:

Data engineers use Python to build and maintain data pipelines, ETL (Extract, Transform, Load) processes, and data warehouses. They work with big data technologies like Apache Spark, Hadoop, and Kafka to process and analyze large volumes of data efficiently. Python's rich ecosystem of libraries and tools makes it well-suited for data engineering tasks.

Cybersecurity:

Python is increasingly used in cybersecurity for tasks such as penetration testing, vulnerability scanning, and security automation. Python developers in this field write scripts and tools to detect security threats, analyze network traffic, and implement security controls. They also contribute to open-source security projects and collaborate with security researchers and analysts.

Academic and Research:

Python is widely used in academia and research for scientific computing, data analysis, and computational research. Python developers in this field work on projects ranging from scientific simulations and modeling to natural language processing and bioinformatics. They contribute to research papers, collaborate with domain experts, and develop software tools for academic and scientific communities.

Freelancing and Consulting:

Many Python developers choose to work as freelancers or consultants, offering their expertise to clients on a project basis. Freelancers may specialize in specific domains or technologies, such as web development, data science, or automation. They have the flexibility to work on diverse projects, set their own schedules, and negotiate their rates.

Entrepreneurship:

Python developers with entrepreneurial ambitions may start their own tech startups or businesses. Python's rapid prototyping capabilities, extensive library ecosystem, and supportive community make it an ideal choice for building innovative products and services. Entrepreneurial Python developers may focus on areas like software as a service (SaaS), mobile apps, e-commerce, or niche markets.

Teaching and Training:

Experienced Python developers often transition into teaching and training roles, sharing their knowledge and expertise with others. They may work as instructors at coding bootcamps, online learning platforms, or educational institutions. Teaching Python allows developers to give back to the community, inspire the next generation of programmers, and contribute to the growth of the tech industry.

As you progress in your Python journey, consider exploring these career paths and opportunities to find the one that aligns best with your interests, skills, and goals. Whether you're passionate about building software applications, analyzing data, securing systems, or teaching others, Python offers a wealth of possibilities for career advancement and personal growth. Continuously learning, adapting, and seizing new opportunities will help you thrive in the dynamic and ever-evolving field of Python development.

Mastery Is a Journey:

As you reach advanced levels of proficiency in Python programming, it's essential to remember that mastery is a journey, not a destination. The world of Python programming is vast and ever-evolving, offering endless opportunities for growth and exploration

Embrace Lifelong Learning:

Mastery in Python, like any skill, requires continuous learning and adaptation. Stay curious and open-minded, always seeking to expand your knowledge and expertise. Explore new libraries, frameworks, and technologies, and don't shy away from challenging yourself with unfamiliar concepts.

Practice Regularly:

Consistent practice is key to maintaining and improving your Python skills. Dedicate time each day or week to coding exercises, personal projects, or participating in coding challenges. This not only reinforces your existing knowledge but also helps you discover new techniques and approaches.

Experiment and Explore:

Python's versatility allows for experimentation across various domains, from web development and data science to machine learning and automation. Take advantage of this flexibility to explore different areas of interest and gain exposure to diverse problem-solving scenarios.

Contribute to Open Source:

Contributing to open-source projects is an excellent way to apply your skills in real-world scenarios, collaborate with other developers, and give back to the community. Whether it's fixing bugs, adding features, or improving documentation, every contribution helps enrich the Python ecosystem.

Stay Updated:

Keep abreast of the latest developments in the Python community, including updates to the language, new libraries, and emerging trends. Follow Python blogs, attend conferences, participate in webinars, and engage with online communities to stay informed and connected.

Network and Collaborate:

Building a strong professional network is invaluable for career growth and opportunities. Attend meetups, join online forums and communities, and connect with fellow Python enthusiasts and industry professionals. Collaboration often leads to new insights, partnerships, and career prospects.

Set Goals and Challenges:

Define clear goals and objectives for your Python journey, whether it's mastering a specific technology, completing a project, or achieving a certification. Break down larger goals into smaller, actionable steps, and challenge yourself to push beyond your comfort zone.

Seek Feedback and Mentorship:

Solicit feedback from peers, mentors, and experienced professionals to gain valuable insights into your code, projects, and career trajectory. Mentorship can provide guidance, support, and accountability as you navigate your Python journey.

Diversify Your Skill Set:

Python proficiency complements a wide range of skills and technologies. Consider expanding your skill set by learning related languages (e.g., JavaScript, SQL), exploring cloud computing platforms (e.g., AWS, Azure), or delving into DevOps practices and tools.

Remain Patient and Persistent:

Mastery takes time and persistence. Be patient with yourself, celebrate your successes, and learn from setbacks and challenges. Stay motivated by focusing on the progress you've made and the exciting opportunities that lie ahead.

Remember, mastery in Python programming is not a destination but a lifelong journey of growth, discovery, and innovation. By embracing curiosity, continuous learning, and a growth mindset, you'll continue to evolve as a proficient and versatile Python developer, contributing to the vibrant and dynamic Python community. Keep practicing, experimenting, and exploring new horizons it's all part of the exhilarating adventure of mastering Python.

THANK YOU:

As we conclude this exploration into the world of Python programming, it's important to reflect on the progress you've made and the skills you've acquired. Whether you're a beginner just starting out or an experienced developer seeking to deepen your expertise, your commitment to mastering Python has brought you closer to your goals.

Throughout this journey, you've encountered challenges, learned new concepts, and expanded your horizons. You've written code, solved problems, and created projects that showcase your abilities as a Python developer. But remember, mastery is not about reaching a final destination - it's about embracing the process of continuous growth and improvement.

As you move forward on your Python journey, keep the following principles in mind:

1. **Stay Curious and Hungry for Knowledge**: The world of Python programming is vast and ever-evolving. Stay curious, explore new ideas, and never stop learning. Embrace challenges as opportunities for growth, and approach each new concept with enthusiasm and determination.

2. **Practice Regularly and Consistently**: Mastery comes through practice and repetition. Dedicate time each day or week to coding exercises, projects, and challenges. By consistently engaging with Python, you'll reinforce your skills and build confidence in your abilities.

3. **Seek Feedback and Learn from Others**: Don't hesitate to seek feedback from peers, mentors, and experienced developers. Embrace constructive criticism as a tool for improvement, and be open to different perspectives and approaches. Remember, collaboration and community are at the heart of Python programming.

4. **Share Your Knowledge and Experience**: As you continue to grow as a Python developer, consider giving back to the community by sharing your knowledge and experiences. Write tutorials, contribute to open-source projects, or mentor aspiring developers. By sharing what you've learned, you'll inspire others and contribute to the collective advancement of the Python ecosystem.

5. **Stay Resilient and Persevere**: The journey to mastery is not without its obstacles and setbacks. Stay resilient in the face of challenges, and persevere through difficulties with determination and grit. Remember that every obstacle is an opportunity to learn and grow stronger.

6. **Celebrate Your Achievements**: Take time to celebrate your achievements and milestones along the way. Whether it's completing a challenging project, mastering a new concept, or reaching a personal goal, acknowledge your progress and recognize the effort you've put in.

As we part ways, know that the journey doesn't end here - it's just the beginning of a lifelong pursuit of excellence in Python programming. Whether you're building applications, solving problems, or pushing the boundaries of what's possible, may your Python journey be filled with discovery, growth, and success.

Thank you once again for joining me on this remarkable journey, and I wish you all the best in your future endeavors. Keep coding, keep learning, and keep pushing the boundaries of what you can achieve with Python. Until we meet again, farewell, and may your Python journey be filled with endless possibilities.

Dr. Hesham Mohamed Elsherif